THE MODERN LANGUAGE ASSOCIATION
OF AMERICA

MONOGRAPH SERIES
XX

THE SOURCES OF THE TEXT OF QUEVEDO'S
POLÍTICA DE DIOS

Approved for Publication in the Monograph Series

The Sources of the Text of Quevedo's

POLÍTICA DE DIOS

by

JAMES O. CROSBY

The MODERN LANGUAGE ASSOCIATION OF AMERICA   *New York, 1959*

TO

AILEEN O'HEA CROSBY

AND

LAURENCE ALDEN CROSBY

PREFACE

I T IS MY hope that the present study will identify the sources of the text of the *Política de Dios* with sufficient clarity to make possible the eventual preparation of both a reliable edition of the text, and a careful stylistic analysis of the author's numerous revisions.

It is a great pleasure to express my sincere gratitude to Professor Revilo P. Oliver, of the University of Illinois, for the generosity with which he offered me learned advice in matters of textual criticism. I am further very grateful to Professor Oliver, and to Professor Elias L. Rivers, of Dartmouth College, for their kindness in reading and criticizing the manuscript of this study. The Graduate College of the University of Illinois supported my work with great generosity, and I am deeply indebted to Thelma Canale-Parola, Merlin H. Forster, and Antonia Griñán for their conscientious assistance in the tasks of transcription, collation and proofreading. Finally, I wish to thank the many European libraries which so kindly offered me information about their collections of the early editions of Quevedo's works. I owe a special debt of gratitude in this connection to Miss Helen M. Welch, of the University of Illinois Library, for the purchase of many rare books related to my work.

JAMES O. CROSBY

University of Illinois
Urbana, Illinois, 1959

CONTENTS

INTRODUCTION

FRANCISCO DE QUEVEDO Y VILLEGAS was born in 1580 and brought up at the Spanish Court, where his father was secretary to Anne of Austria, Philip II's fourth Queen. At the turn of the century he began his literary career, and by 1613 had already produced some of his best-known poetry and satirical prose, including such works as the *Buscón,* four of the *Sueños,* and a series of sonnets on death. The next six years Quevedo spent in the service of a close friend, the Duke of Osuna, Viceroy of Sicily and later of Naples. As the Ambassador of Naples, and as Osuna's personal representative at the Spanish Court, he had an opportunity to see at first hand the internal corruption and venality which pervaded the government early in the seventeenth century, and to reflect upon the awful responsibility incurred by Philip III in allowing his greedy and ambitious favorites to usurp royal prerogatives and plunder the national treasury.

Quevedo is not known to have done any serious literary work while active in politics, and indeed his correspondence is eloquent testimony of the extent to which he was involved rather in an unremitting turmoil of negotiations, interviews, state functions, and appearances before the royal councils, to say nothing of annual trips between Naples and Madrid. In the summer of 1619, however, he left Osuna's service, retiring temporarily to his estate at La Torre de Juan Abad, in La Mancha. It was his custom to write while at La Torre, and it is probable that the First Part of the *Política de Dios,* completed early in 1621, was written there (the dedication to the Count-duke of Olivares was signed April 5, 1621, in La Torre).[1]

[1] The usually accepted theory that Quevedo began writing the *Política* as early as 1617 is based on his vague and general reference to "diez años ha," found in the ingratiating Dedication to the Count-duke of Olivares (*Política,* Madrid, 1626, f. [2r]). Various studies documenting Quevedo's trying and time-consuming activities for Osuna between 1617 and 1619 are listed in my article, "Noticias y documentos de Quevedo,

1

In such works as the *Buscón* and the *Sueños,* Quevedo had combined parody and satire in an effort to criticize the corrupt social customs of his time. Almost every chapter of the First Part of the *Política de Dios* contains lively if not violent criticism of the excesses of ambitious favorites, and of the moral and political irresponsibility of pusillanimous kings. It is a logical inference that this treatise, written during the last two years of Philip III's reign, was directed against the King and his favorites, and expresses in a sense Quevedo's moral and patriotic indignation at what Philip's government was doing to his country.

The theme of the relationship between monarch and favorite, which Quevedo treated extensively in the First Part of the *Política de Dios,* was to become one of his predilections, and was to be set forth at length in such later works as the *Discurso de todos los diablos,* the *Vida de Marco Bruto,* and *La fortuna con seso y la hora de todos.* And although in the long Second Part of the *Política de Dios,* written between 1634 and 1639, a variety of political topics are introduced, the theme of the favorite remains by far the most important.

While Quevedo wrote several works which deal in whole or in part with political questions, the *Política de Dios* is his only major treatise of this sort (the *Marco Bruto* is a running commentary on a consecutive series of direct quotations from Plutarch). Scholars generally agree that the *Política* occupies a prominent position among the numerous political treatises produced in Spain in the seventeenth century.[2] As José Antonio

---

1616-1617," *Hispanófila,* II, no. 1 (1958), 3, note 1. On the date of Quevedo's temporary retirement, see Ciriaco Pérez Bustamente, "Quevedo, diplomático," *Revista de Estudios Políticos,* XIII (año V, 1945), 180-182.

[2] Donald W. Bleznik, "La *Política de Dios* de Quevedo y el pensamiento político en el Siglo de Oro," *Nueva Revista de Filología Hispánica,* IX (1955), 385. Aside from books and articles on the *Política* itself (partial bibliography in Bleznik, p. 385, nn. 1, 2), it is mentioned prominently in histories of Spanish political thought (see note 3 below), and in such studies as John C. Dowling, *El pensamiento político-filosófico de Saavedra Fajardo* (Murcia, 1957), esp. pp. 281-290, and Francisco Murillo Ferrol, *Saavedra Fajardo y la política del barroco* (Madrid, 1957), pp. 20 ff.

Maravall has pointed out, these treatises were not formal, systematic analyses designed for theologians and philosophers, but rather practical guides in the art of ruling, addressed to kings and ministers. And since the political writers of this time wrote in the vernacular for a lay audience which they wished to captivate rather than to confute, they neglected weighty argumentation and formal presentation, in favor of short discourses enhanced by various literary and stylistic devices.[3] In the case of the *Política de Dios,* the teachings of Christ and the example of His life, especially in relation to the Apostles, are applied directly to the moral, political, and administrative problems of a seventeenth-century monarch. The result is a well-argued series of analogies, some more plausible than others, but all couched in bold language and laced with thinly-veiled criticism of Philip III and his favorites.

A text of this sort by a major writer is naturally of fundamental importance. Moreover, the fact that it exists in two very different versions (one of them almost wholly unpublished) is also of interest: both were written by the author himself, and a comparison of the two would undoubtedly reveal much about his ideas, his style (in almost all of the connotations of the word), and his motives for revising the text.

But the *Política* cannot be the subject of a critical or stylistic analysis because no edition sufficiently reliable to meet the demands of modern scholarship has been available.[4] Nor could

[3] José Antonio Maravall, *Teoría española del estado en el siglo XVII* (Madrid, 1944), pp. 19-45. The ideas expressed in this penetrating and comprehensive study are accepted in Juan Beneyto Pérez' equally excellent *Historia de las doctrinas políticas* (Madrid, 1950), pp. 330-339.

[4] The modern edition of Quevedo's works, edited by Luis Astrana Marín, has aroused severe criticism from such scholars as José Manuel Blecua (*NRFH* VIII, 1954, p. 156), Américo Castro (*RFE* XXI, 1934, p. 178), Miguel Herrero García *(Rev. de la Bibl., Arch. y Museo,* XIV, 1945, p. 367), and Juan Antonio Tamayo (*Bol. de la Bibl. de Menéndez Pelayo,* XXI, 1945, p. 456). For further documentation on Astrana Marín's repeated and serious errors in the transcription of texts, see my articles in *PMLA* LXXI (1956), 1120, n. 17; *HR* XXIII (1955), 270, n. 33; *MLN* LXX (1955), 519, n. 3; *MLQ* XVII (1956), 105, n. 11; *Hispanófila* II, no. 1 (1958), nn. 5, 9, 13, 18, 46; *Bol. de la Bibl. de Menéndez Pelayo*

4 *Introduction*

there be any attempt at such an edition, because the complex history of the text prior to the author's final revision has remained largely unknown. Until this tradition is established, no one can know which text or texts to edit.

It is my purpose in the present study to define this tradition by sorting out the mass of different manuscript and printed sources of the *Política,* adducing several new texts and establishing the filiation of all. Since little work of this sort has been done on seventeenth-century Spanish literature, my methods are those which have been used in similar studies of large groups of Classical, English and Old French texts.[5]

Although the First Part of the *Política de Dios* was completed in 1621, the oldest and purest text known to exist today dates

XXXIV (1958), p. 235, n. 2; p. 240, n. 1; p. 244, n. 1; p. 253, n. 1. Although the titlepage of Astrana's edition proclaims it to be "critical," and based on "textos genuinos del autor," the editor himself states in the Prologue (*Obras completas: obras en verso,* by Quevedo, Madrid, 1943, p. l), that he took his text of the *Política* from the edition published nearly a century ago by Aureliano Fernández-Guerra (Madrid, 1867-1868, 2 vols). Fernández-Guerra was the greatest pioneer in Quevedo studies, but he unfortunately belonged to an age which accepted as a matter of course such questionable practices as the suppression of variants, the eclectic conflation of different versions, and the silent emendation and "modernization" of the syntax as well as the orthography of seventeenth-century texts.

[5] See, for example, Robert K. Root, *The Textual Tradition of Chaucer's "Troilus"* (Oxford University Press, 1916); Aubrey Diller, *The Tradition of the Minor Greek Geographers* (American Philological Association, 1952); Alexander Turyn, *The Byzantine Manuscript Tradition of the Tragedies of Euripedes* (University of Illinois Press, 1957); E. B. Ham, *Textual Criticism and Jehan le Venelais* (University of Michigan Press, 1946); Sir Walter Greg, *The Editorial Problem in Shakespeare: A Survey of the Foundations of the Text* (Oxford University Press, 1942); T. H. Bowyer, *A Bibliographical Examination of the Earliest Editions of the Letters of Junius* (University of Virginia Press, 1958). Since writing these lines, two studies of the theory of textual criticism have come to my attention: E. B. Ham, "Textual Criticism and Common Sense," *Romance Philology* XII (1959), 198-215, and Vinton A. Dearing, *A Manual of Textual Analysis,* to be published shortly by the University of California Press at Berkeley. The theoretical principles used in the present study are classified analytically in the Index below. See also the Intro. and Index of the study cited below in Chap. I, n. 6.

from 1626. This manuscript was once the property of the Duke of Frías, and, although lost to scholars since 1852, has just now been recovered. The first printed edition of the *Política* also dates from 1626, and was published in Zaragoza by a bookseller who stated that it was appearing without the author's consent. It has generally been believed that this edition was represented by copies in the Biblioteca Nacional de Madrid and the Biblioteca Universitaria de Zaragoza, but as may be seen in the chapters which follow, we now know this is not so. The true first edition is a text heretofore unknown.

To the best of my knowledge the *Política* was reprinted more often in the first year of its publication than any other contemporary Spanish book, including Cervantes' popular *Quijote*. (In the spring of 1626, for instance, editions appeared at the rate of one every six weeks, and in the fall, at the rate of one every month; since seventeenth-century printers usually ran off about 1500 copies of any edition,[6] some 12,000 copies of the *Política* must have been printed in Spain in 1626 alone.) It is now possible to document the impact which this treatise had when it first appeared in print, and to identify at least some of the reasons for its unusual popularity.

In the chapters which follow, the Frías manuscript is treated first, even though this means that its relationship to the first edition is discussed before that edition is formally identified. I have chosen this sequence because the manuscript is the earliest and most pure text, and because it seems best to avoid, insofar as is possible, a mixed discussion of manuscripts and printed editions. The first edition is much more closely related to the second and third editions than it is to any other text, and so to reserve the manuscript for a second chapter would be to disturb the chronological order of the discussion, and to send the reader back to the manuscript after he had finished with the third edition. Finally, I believe it is possible to discuss the manu-

---

[6] Agustín González de Amezúa y Mayo, "Cómo se hacía un libro en nuestro Siglo de Oro," in his *Opúsculos histórico-literarios* (Madrid, 1951), I, 352.

script and the first edition in Chapter I without reference to the complex typographical and bibliographical characteristics which distinguish the first edition from other printed texts.

In the Frías manuscript and in the early Zaragoza editions, the text of the *Política* was divided into twenty chapters with the tripartite title *Política de Dios, gobierno de Cristo, tiranía de Satanás.* I have called this text the "early version." As copies circulated in Spain, a certain amount of sharp criticism arose which offended Quevedo so much that he repudiated this version, and brought out a thoroughly revised text. In this "authorized version," published in Madrid in 1626, he reduced the title to *Política de Dios, gobierno de Cristo,* inserted three new chapters, and renumbered the others to bring the total to twenty-four. He also introduced literally hundreds of alterations in the text, which range from simple rewording to the omission or insertion of lengthy paragraphs, and which were prompted by various es-thetic, stylistic, political, and religious considerations. Such a set of alterations often reveals a wealth of illuminating detail about the creative processes of a writer, provided one possesses the precise text on which the revisions were made. In the case of the First Part of the *Política,* it is now possible to identify this text.

As mentioned above, the Second Part of the *Política* was written between 1634 and 1639. Two versions exist, one in an early manuscript and the other in the posthumous first edition of the Second Part (Madrid, 1655). These two versions differ widely: the edition contains a text twice as long as the manu-script, and even the chapters shared by both do not appear in anything like the same order. Hundreds of smaller differences also appear, some of which can be proved to be changes intro-duced after 1654, when Quevedo had been dead nine years.

As in the case of the First Part, no reliable edition exists of these texts. Careful analysis has clarified their relationships, and provided a sound basis for the future preparation of both an edition, and a detailed critical study of the author's alterations.

I

THE EARLY VERSION IN THE FRÍAS MANUSCRIPT

A CENTURY AGO Aureliano Fernández-Guerra devoted a number of years to the enormous task of collecting, classifying, and editing the works of Quevedo. The result was the discovery of many new MSS and editions, the first classification of this mass of source material, and a monumental edition of Quevedo's prose (*Biblioteca de Autores Españoles,* Vols. XXIII, 1852, and XLVIII, 1859).

In the first volume of his edition, Fernández-Guerra printed a description of a MS of the *Política de Dios* which was at that time owned by the Duke of Frías (see full bibliographical description below in Appendix II). Fernández-Guerra described the titlepage and the preliminaries of this MS, mentioned the total number of leaves (125), and with neither explanation nor documentation said of the handwriting, "letra del amanuense de Quevedo," and of the text "Todo, menos en las erratas de imprenta, igual a la impresión de Zaragoza" (*BAE* XXIII, p. cxiii). Although he accepted Quevedo's statement that the *Política* was printed in Zaragoza "sin mi asistencia y sabiduría" (*BAE* XXIII, p. 3, 8), he also said, without any explanation, that "en nuestra publicación [i.e., edición] hemos tenido a la vista el manuscrito facilitado por el mismo Quevedo a Roberto Duport para la edición primera de Zaragoza" (p. 5). And in spite of the statement to the effect that the text of the MS was utilized, there do not appear in Fernández-Guerra's edition any of the very numerous variants of the MS, which thus remained completely unpublished.

Since the appearance of Fernández-Guerra's description in 1852, nothing has been known of the Frías MS of the *Política*

7

de Dios. At the turn of the century, Menéndez y Pelayo began the publication of Quevedo's works, but his edition remained unfinished, and so does not contain any reference to this MS. More recently, Astrana Marín has limited himself to copying part, but not all, of Fernández-Guerra's notes.[1] A few years ago, however, the present writer had the good fortune to acquire this MS of the *Política de Dios,* which had passed from the library of the Duke of Frías to that of Fernández-Guerra, and upon his death, to his heir, Luis Valdés.

A. THE UNITY OF THE MS AND THE FIRST EDITION

An analysis of the text of the Frías MS discloses a surprising similarity to the first edition of the *Política de Dios* (Zaragoza, 1626).[2] As may be seen in the bibliographical description in Appendix II, this similarity is perhaps more easily discovered in the titlepage and preliminaries than in the corpus of the text. Except for three variants, the titlepages of the MS and the edition are identical with respect to the text, the general arrangement of the paragraphs, and even the position of the design.[3] With the exception of a short *licencia,* the two texts contain the same preliminary material, and in the same order.

All of this means that on the titlepage of the MS there appear the words "con licencia," together with the name of the printer

---

[1] Luis Astrana Marín, ed. Quevedo, *Obras completas: obras en verso* (Madrid, 1943), p. 1303b, no. 167, "Catálogo de manuscritos." This edition and its companion volume, *Obras completas en prosa* (Madrid, 1945), are hereinafter cited respectively as *Verso* and *Prosa.* Menéndez y Pelayo's edition was entitled *Obras completas* (Seville, Bibliófilos Andaluces, 1897).

[2] As explained in the Introduction, the identification of the hitherto unknown first edition has been left for Chapter II, while in Chapter I, the discussion of the MS and the first edition has been handled, satisfactorily I hope, without reference to the complex typographical and bibliographical characteristics which distinguish the first edition from other printed texts.

[3] The three variants are found in the title (MS: "Christo, y Tyranía"; first edition: "Christo: Tyranía"), in the date (MS: 1625; edition: 1626), and in the last line of the titlepage, which is lacking in the MS (edition: "A costa de Roberto Duport, Mercader de Libros").

and the place and date of publication of the edition, and in the preliminaries an *aprobación,* a *licencia para imprimir,* the author's statement entitled "A quien lee," and a letter from the publisher, Roberto Duport, to the reader, in which Duport explains why "I am printing" ("doy a la estampa") this book.

The relationship between the MS and the first edition is further defined by a series of passages which are found in all texts save these two, and which exceed the usual length of variants introduced in the transmission of seventeenth-century texts. The following examples may be cited (the passages missing in the MS and the first edition appear below in square brackets):

En el libro de Talmud Berachot, que quiere deçir 'De las vendiçiones,' capítulo Hen Vndin, ['No estarán,' dize Rabbi Eliazar, 'desde el día que el Templo se destruyó;'] dice el Hebreo 'Sarei Tefilo,' 'Las puertas de la oración se cerraron' (MS p. 18; first edition f. 7v; Astrana, *Prosa,* Chap. ii, p. 382a, but with this passage omitted).

Christo . . . ya los auía dicho que conuenía que cada vno tomase su cruz, y le siguiesse, . . . pero esto del padecer, y del morir, quicre que sea quando en su ausençia y en su lugar gouiernen; aora son súbditos, padezca el Maestro y la caueza: [quando temporalmente le succedieron, y cada vno assistió el gouierno de su prouincia,] quien aquí, siendo obejas, los desuía la mala palabra, . . . quando sean pastores, los embiará el cuchillo (MS pp. 108-109; ed. f. 39v; *Prosa* x, p. 399a).

Por los delinquentes se han de haçer fineças. [¿Quién padeció por el bueno?] Con estas palabras habló elegantemente la charidad del Apóstol San Pablo (MS p. 41; ed. f. 15v; *Prosa* iii, p. 386a).

¿Quién más en desgraçia de Dios que el Demonio? [¿Que vna legión de ellos?] Criatura desconoçida, vasallo aleuoso, que se amotinó contra Dios (MS p. 36; ed. f. 14r; *Prosa* iii, p. 385a).[4]

[4] In order to facilitate the reading of these and other quotations, which are designed for semantic rather than linguistic analysis, I have modernized the capitalization, accentuation, and, cautiously, the punctuation. Abbreviations have been resolved, and words run together have been separated ('ysus,' 'aesta,' 'apedir,' etc.). I quote whenever possible from the MS, or, in discussions of printed texts only, from the earliest edition involved in any particular passage, and since there are no modern editions of these texts, I include citations from Astrana, *Prosa* (although the primitive errors do not appear in this edition, the reader will at least

There are three more passages similar to these, making a total of seven omissions common only to the MS and the first edition.[5]

In addition to the above passages, two are found in the MS and the first edition, but not in any other seventeenth-century text (the passages in question appear below in square brackets): "Sólo resta que . . . los castigue y alexe de sí, y no será [disculpa decir que no se atreuerán], antes temerlo es religión" (MS pp. 171-172; ed. f. 63r; *Prosa* xix, p. 416b-417a). . . . "Le procuró tapar la voca con la puñada [que le dio], y dar a la verdad tósigo" (MS p. 210; ed. f. 78r; *Prosa* xxiii, p. 424b).

Normally, the presence in several texts of two passages like those last quoted indicates a certain textual relationship brought about by transmission, not by coincidence.[6] Although the converse is not so easy to demonstrate (it may be theoretically impossible to prove conclusively that the lack of a few passages in two or more texts is not due to coincidence), it is very unlikely that coincidence could produce a series of seven omissions as lengthy and as uniform as those quoted first above and in note 5.

The evidence that the MS and the first edition are closely related is supported by five manifest errors and at least two cases of *lectio difficilior,* all of which appear only in these two

---

be able to examine their context, and, with the chapter numbers, locate the citation in any of the repaginated printings of Astrana's edition). It should be said that since Astrana's edition by his own admission is little more than a copy of Fernández-Guerra's text (see *Verso,* "Introduction," p. lb), it contains the latter's silent emendations and interpolations, some of which appear in the passages quoted in this and other chapters.

[5] For the three other passages, compare Astrana's text with the MS, which reads as follows: "escogió doce hombres, vno le vendió" (MS p. 21; ed. f. 8v; *Prosa* ii, p. 382a); "vno de sus discípulos, Iudas, que le auía de vender" (MS p. 52; ed. f. 19v; *Prosa* v, p. 388a); "Y vino Iesvs a Hierusalém, y como entrasse en el Templo" (MS p. 170; ed. f. 62v; *Prosa* xix, p. 416b). In the last example, Astrana follows Fernández-Guerra's silent emendation; the text of the old editions, except the first, reads as follows: "Y entró Iesús en el Templo en Ierusalém, y como entrasse en el Templo . . ."

[6] For an example of the application of this principle to a group of texts, see Chapter II of my study *The Text Tradition of the* Memorial *"Católica, sacra, real Magestad"* (Univ. of Kansas Press, Lawrence, Kansas, 1958).

texts.[7] Examples of the errors follow (my corrections are in square brackets):

Nos dexó exemplo en muchas de sus obras, y en particular en el paralytico, deteniendo [detenido] treinta y ocho años en aquel soportal por falta de hombre (MS, f. [9r]; ed. f. [7v]; *Prosa*, letter from Vander Hammen, p. 1684b).

Acceptatores [Acceptores] vultus (MS p. 35; ed. f. 13v; *Prosa* iii, p. 385a).

Nadie le ha de tocar que no lo sienta, que no sepa que le toca, que no dé a entender que no lo saue [que lo saue] (MS p. 48; ed. f. 18r; *Prosa* iv, p. 387a).

Ego baptizo in aqua; medicus [medius] autem vestrum stetit, quem vos nescitis (MS p. 147; ed. f. 54r; *Prosa* xvii, p. 412a).[8]

It seems clear that the MS and the first edition are two very closely related texts, a circumstance which operates to conceal

---

[7] In addition, the MS and the first edition share 20 more errors, but since these 20 also appear in various other editions, they are not evidence of the unity of the MS and the first edition.

[8] In the remaining error the Greek word 'Aprosopolepsia,' written in roman letters, is missing in the MS, and misplaced and misspelled in the edition (MS p. 35; ed. f. 13v; *Prosa* iii, p. 384b). The cases of *lectio difficilior* referred to above are found in two passages dealing with Saint John the Baptist (the readings of the editions other than the first are in square brackets): "Tu quis es? Et confessus est, et non negauit, et confessus est: Quia non sum ego Christus. Pondera repetidamente que confessó que no era el vngido, el embiado, que no era Christo, y dícelo dos veçes por cosa (aun quen [aun en] San Juan) digna de grande admiración" (MS pp. 146-147; ed. f. 53v; *Prosa* xvii, p. 411b; Quevedo here points out that in John i. 19-20, the Evangelist repeats something twice because, even though Saint John the Baptist said it and not Christ, it is worthy of note). "La inquietud y juguetes de vnos pies deshonestos tuuo por precio de su descompostura la cabeça del precursor, postre de vn banquete y premio de vn bayle, auiendo sido su pompa el desierto, su exército [exercicio] la penitencia, y llamábasse voz que gritaba en desierto" (MS p. 156; ed. f. 57r; *Prosa* xvii, p. 413b). The MS and the first edition also share exclusively two examples of 'seguito,' evidently a primitive or corrupt form of 'séquito' (MS pp. 21, 92; ed. ff. 8v, 33r; *Prosa* ii, ix, pp. 382a, 395b). Since 'seguito' may be an Italianism (comp. it. 'seguito,' 'seguitare,' and Joan Corominas, *Diccionario crítico-etimológico*, s.v. 'seguir'), or perhaps the result of the influence of the Spanish 'seguir,' it cannot be considered a manifest error. But its presence in two different passages in both the MS and the first edition, and in no other text, would seem to indicate a close relationship between the MS and the first edition. The only other example of 'seguito' known to me is quoted in Chapter II, n. 6.

their respective sources from anything but a detailed examination.

B. THE MS NOT THE SOURCE OF THE FIRST EDITION

Although it has been suggested that the MS was the immediate source of the text of the first edition,[9] it is doubtful that this was so. The MS has the general appearance of a volume prepared with care and bound much more artistically than would be the case in a text prepared for a printer (see in Appendix II the description of the gilded designs on the covers). The pages contain none of the official rubrics specified by the laws governing printing in seventeenth-century Spain,[10] and no compositors' marks at all (not even the usual lines to indicate the end of each printed page).

Furthermore, one of the two *licencias* which appear in the first edition is lacking in the MS, as is the following passage in the text (the missing words appear in square brackets): "Christo dice que su cabeca[11] no se inclina; [no es cabeça en el pueblo de Christo la que se inclina;] el lo diçe y lo enseña" (MS p. 114; ed. f. 42r; *Prosa* x, p. 400b). This is a typical example of haplography: the eye of the scribe jumped from the first 'inclina' to the second, omitting the intervening clause. Haplography appears frequently in the transmission of texts; moreover, the scribe who copied out the MS of the *Politica* had a special tendency to make this type of error.[12] Since the example quoted above does not

---

[9] Fernández-Guerra, *BAE* XXIII, 5.

[10] See Agustín González de Amezúa y Mayo, "Cómo se hacía un libro en nuestro Siglo de Oro," in his *Opúsculos histórico-literarios* (Madrid, 1951), I, 335.

[11] Although perhaps the scribe was inclined to use the cedilla when the letter *c* was followed by *a* or *o,* there are many cases of *c* in such a position without the cedilla. *c* followed by *a:* 'cabeca' (6 examples), 'cabeça' (7); 'grandeca', 'grandeça'; 'agonicando,' 'agoniçaba'; 'singularica,' 'naturaleca,' 'riqueças,' 'desembaraçada,' 'bonança,' 'pobreça.' *c* followed by o: 'hico,' 'hiço'; 'forcoso,' 'forçoso'; 'abraço,' 'coraçón,' 'embaraçó,' 'açote,' 'raçonamiento.' The use of the cedilla when *c* is followed by *e* or *i* is also irregular: 'cielo,' 'çielo'; 'licencia,' 'liçençia,' etc.

[12] In various deletions which appear in the MS one can see how the scribe has skipped backward to repeat words (dittography) or forward to

involve any manifest error, a compositor who had before his eyes only this text would not be prompted to emend it. In other words, if the first edition had been made directly from the MS, it is almost certain that the words missing in the MS would not have been inserted into the edition because the compositor would not have seen any need for such an emendation. The fact that this passage and the *licencia* mentioned above appear in the first edition, would suggest that the edition was made from a text which also contained these two items, and not from the MS.

Further evidence of the source of the first edition can be found in a series of five palimpsest readings in the MS, in which the scribe emended his first transcription, almost as soon as he had made it, by writing the correct words or letters over what he had previously set down.[13] Examples follow (I quote the text as it

---

omit others (haplography), and then, upon realizing his error, crossed out the repeated words. In the example cited above, the repetition of a word in the text brought about the error; in others, it was brought about by the suggestion of the syntax (a transition, the expected introduction of a subordinate clause, a pair of parallel constructions, two negatives, etc.). Examples follow (in square brackets, the deletions): "Si la horca fuera sólo para las personas, y no para los delitos, no tuuieran otro fin los pobres y desualidos, ni [tuuieran otro] fuera castigo, sino desdicha" (MS p. 89; *Prosa* ix, p. 395a; here the repetition of the negative occasioned the error, which was immediately deleted). At times the scribe omitted what may have seemed to him to be the second of two parallel verbs: "De la carne de su carne, y de los huesos de sus huesos deue recelarse, [porque no] y tener sospecha, porque no se dexe vençer de alguna presumpción mañosa" (MS p. 25; *Prosa* ii, p. 383a). At other times, a transition apparently caused the error: "Pues señor, no es seueridad de mi ingenio, o mala condiçión de mi maliçia; ¡no tengo parte en este raçonamiento! [Quien cudicia el oro y la plata, es ladrón, a robar vino] San Pablo pronunçia estas palabras: 'Quien cudiçia el oro y la plata es ladrón, a robar vino, no entró por la puerta' " (MS p. 191; *Prosa* xxi, p. 420b). Further examples in the MS, pp. 15, 16, 42, 66, 105, 113, 126, 133, 182, 201, and 210.

[13] The superimposed corrections are not large or heavy marks by a rough hand; they are as small and neat as any other letters in the MS (see plates). Close scrutiny of these palimpsest readings under a high-powered magnifying glass, and again under ultra-violet light, has revealed that the characteristics of the ink and the handwriting of the corrections are indistinguishable from those of the rest of the text.

was first written, with the deleted letters in *italics;* after these letters, I repeat the particular word in square brackets, printing in **boldface type** the letters which the scribe superimposed on what he had first written):

Entonces fue Christo lleuado al desierto por el Spíritu, para que fuese tentado del Diablo. . . . Entró Satanás, viendo retirado a Christo, a negociar con él. . . . Tres memoriales traxo para despachar. . . . El primer memorial que despachó fue que hiciesse de las piedras pan. . . . El segundo negocio que pretend*o* **yo** [pretend**ió**] despachar fue . . . (the deletion in the final sentence is found in the MS on p. 195; ed. ff. 72v-73r; *Prosa* xxii, p. 421b).

Rey que pelea y trabaja delante de los suyos, oblígalos a ser valientes. . . . Quien los manda pelear, y no los vee, ése los disculpa de lo que dexaren de haçer. . . . Differentes exerçiç*ios* [exérçitos] son los que pagan los príncipes, que los que acompañan; los vnos trahen grandes gastos, los otros grandes victorias (MS pp. 64-65; ed. ff. 23r-23v; *Prosa* vi, p. 390a).

Mandar al fuego[14] que vaje del çielo, escondid*o* [escondida] tiene alguna presumpçión (MS p. 78; ed. f. 28r; *Prosa* vii, p. 392b).

In the first example quoted, the scribe wrote 'pretendo yo,' then saw the error in the use of the first person singular, and corrected it by writing over his original mistake. In the second example, Quevedo is clearly speaking of the duty of a prince to lead his army in person during a war, and so the scribe corrected the meaningless 'exerçiçios.' In the last example, the position of the adjective 'escondida' immediately after the preceding substantive clause and separated from the noun it modifies by the principal verb, suggested at first that 'escondida' agreed with 'fuego,' or with the preceding clause, whereas the context demands that it agree with 'presumpçión.'

In these three passages, and in two others, the first edition carries the erroneous reading, which remained uncorrected until the appearance of the Madrid edition revised by the author.[15]

[14] I here correct an error in the MS, which reads "Mãdar al çielo."

[15] In one of the two other passages, a quotation from the New Testament which reads "Cum autem dormirent homines, venit inimicus eius, et superseminauit zizania in medio tritici," is translated in the MS as

Palimpsest reading, Frías MS. An example of the dangers of the criterion of style in determining filiation (See Ch.I,n.15)

Palimpsest reading, Frías MS

Palimpsest reading, Frías MS

If the first edition had been made from the MS, it would be
almost impossible to explain why in these passages the compositor, on seeing a superimposed corrected reading, would
search beneath this for an erroneous reading, in order to insert
it into the edition which he was setting up. (In four of the five
passages, the small size of the handwriting of the MS, and the
blots of ink occasioned by the deletions, make the letters underneath quite difficult to decipher without a magnifying glass.) In
my opinion, these palimpsest readings are almost conclusive

---

follows: "El Padre de familias, luego que se durmió, dio lugar a los
malos para que emb*i*assen [*s*embrassen] en su heredad zicaña" (MS p.
115; ed. f. 42r; *Prosa* x, p. 401a; on 'zicaña' without the cedilla, see note
11 above). The other passage is as follows: "Palabras tan llenas que
luego a la vista representan la importancia del sagrado texto. . . . No
sólo en él se halla*n* [halla] la polytica, pero también la economía, la
mediçina, la hystoria, la retórica, la poesía, la iurisprudencia, y otras tales"
(MS f. [6r]; ed. f. [5v]; *Prosa,* letter from Vander Hammen, p. 1683a).
In this passage, 'halla' agrees only with 'polytica,' and in the next clause
("pero también . . .") 'halla' is understood, with its number changed, by a
type of anacoluthon common in the seventeenth century. Finally, there
is in the MS a deletion of a reading which, though not an error, seems
to belong to the class of deletions under discussion: "Y para más fuerça
el *proprio* [mismo] Christo se apropria este título de rey" (MS p. 16;
ed, f. 7r; *Prosa* ii, p. 381b). The first edition reads here 'proprio,' but
when the copyist of the MS reached the word 'apropria' later in the same
clause, he noticed that it was a paronym, and evidently decided to "improve" the style, changing 'proprio' to 'mismo.' It is interesting to note
that paronyms are found frequently in the Golden Age, which indicates
that their use was not always considered a defect: see a series of examples
from the *Lazarillo de Tormes* listed by Gustav Siebenmann, *Über Sprach
und Stil im "Lazarillo de Tormes"* (Bern, 1953), pp. 81-84 (*Romanica
Helvetica*, XLIII). Of the numerous examples of paronyms in Cervantes,
a few may be found in the *Novelas ejemplares,* ed. F. Rodríguez Marín
(Madrid, Clásicos Castellanos, 1948 and 1943), I, 240, 265, 322; II, 11,
15, 16(2), 33, 41, 190(2), 225, 230, 238, 244, 274. The passage in the
MS of the *Política* is one more example of the real dangers inherent in
any attempt to establish the filiation of old texts by the criterion of style:
the oldest and most authentic version of a text is not necessarily composed of a selection of such variants as may seem to be "better" or
"superior" or more authentic to a twentieth-century editor, and furthermore, even such stylistic practices as usually characterize seventeenth-
century texts are not always found with sufficient regularity to be of use
in determining filiation.

proof that the text of the first edition was not copied from the MS.

An examination of the texts of the MS and the first edition reveals that they share 25 identical manifest errors. (A certain proportion of these 25, and of other groups listed below, were passed on to other editions, and while this would affect any attempt to determine the unique unity of the MS and the first edition, it does not affect the determination of the relationship between these two texts alone.) To these 25 common errors, the MS adds some 56 which do not appear in the edition, and the edition adds about 73.[16] While these figures indicate that the MS is a purer text than the edition, they hardly offer a numerical difference sufficiently wide to serve as the basis for definite conclusions about the filiation of the two texts. Sometimes it is possible to prove that most of the errors in one of two texts are of a superficial type, easy to discover and correct, while those of the other are serious and more difficult to correct (examples are discussed below in section C of this chapter, and in section B of Chapter II). In the MS and the first edition, however, the same proportion of serious errors is found in both texts (27 and 35, respectively, out of 56 and 73).[17]

A different analysis of the corrected errors shows that of a total of 81 errors found in the MS, the edition corrects 56, or almost 66 per cent. In other editions of the *Política* published in the same year by the same printer, this percentage is between 40 and 50, which suggests that, had the first edition been made

[16] My figures are approximate because it is not always easy to distinguish between an error and a variant, to say nothing of an error and a case of *lectio difficilior,* and I therefore hesitate to state that there can be neither more nor less than precisely 56 errors in the MS and 73 in the edition. Although the possibility of arriving at an erroneous figure is not great when dealing with a very few errors found equally in a large number of texts, the difficulty increases when one deals with numerous errors in a single text.

[17] The 35 are those which passed from the first to the second edition undetected by the compositor of the second edition (that is to say, they were relatively difficult to discover and correct); the 27 represent those in the MS which seem to me to be of the same type as the 35.

from the MS, an unusually large number of errors would have been corrected. (Conversely, the fact that of a total of 98 errors in the edition, the MS corrected 73, or just over 73 per cent, provides evidence that the MS was not copied directly from the edition.)

The general appearance of the MS, the lack of the *licencia* which appears in the edition, and the unusually high rate of correction of errors support the theory that the MS was not the source of the first edition. I believe that conclusive proof is provided by the example of haplography and the five palimpsest readings.

C. THE MS NOT A COPY OF THE FIRST EDITION

In defining the relationship between the MS and the first edition, it is necessary to examine the possibility that the former is a copy of the latter.

As has already been mentioned, the two texts share 25 identical manifest errors, to which the edition adds some 73 other errors which are not found in the MS. Many of these last errors are of a type difficult to correct and therefore prone to be transmitted, and it is important to note that while none appear in the MS, many are quite similar to others which do so appear. The following are examples of errors which do not appear in the MS, but do appear in the first edition and in five or more editions copied directly or indirectly from the first (my corrections are in square brackets):

Celebraréle [Celebraránle] siempre como deben a v.m. y a su ingenio propios y estraños (ed. f. [9v]; *Prosa,* letter from Vander Hammen, p. 1686a).

A los Reyes . . . los conuiene no sólo *no* dar el primer lugar a la voluntad, pero ninguna [ninguno]; han de hazer la voluntad de Dios solamente (ed. f. 3v; *Prosa* i, p. 379b——I supply *'no'*).

Aunque las sinagogas del pueblo endurecidos [endurecido] le apropiaron el reyno (ed. f. 7v; *Prosa ii,* p. 381b).

De las piedras se podían [podía] hazer pan (ed. ff. 27v-28r; *Prosa* vii, p. 392b).

Non solum qui ea faciunt ea [qui faciunt ea], sed etiam qui consentiunt facientibus (ed. f. 78v; *Prosa* xxiii, p. 425a).

In the first example, the separation of the verb from its subject, combined with the general context of the preceding sentence, brought about the error in the person and number of the verb. In the second and fourth examples, and perhaps the third, the proximity of a preceding noun influenced the gender of 'ninguno' and the number of 'endurecido' and of 'podía.' Although the final example is a simple instance of dittography, the repetition is of a kind that would not be immediately apparent to one who did not know Latin. Because these errors involve syntax or context, or both, they are much less likely to be corrected than others which are obvious typographical or orthographical blunders, such as 'ptetendió' for 'pretendió' (first edition, f. [5r]), 'codica' for 'codicia' (f. 7v), 'durme' for 'duerme' (f. 40r), 'leuguage' for 'lenguage' (f. 49r), 'teniando' for 'teniendo' (f. 69v), 'sar' for 'ser' (f. 75v), 'menemérito' for 'benemérito' (f. 79v).[18]

As mentioned above in section B, the MS, if it had been copied directly from the first edition, would have corrected over 73 per cent of the 98 errors in the edition, an unusually high percentage. It now appears that many of these errors are of a type not usually corrected. Such data suggest that the MS was not copied from the first edition.

The date on the titlepage of the MS is 1625, while in the edition it is 1626 (see section A above). The last *licencia* of the edition is dated February 23, 1626, which indicates that the edition did not appear until after that date. If the MS had been copied directly from this edition it would be difficult to understand how a scribe, working after February 23, 1626, from an edition with a titlepage and preliminaries dated that same year,

---

[18] There are of course some syntactical errors which are obvious, and therefore easily corrected: 'la obejas' for 'las obejas' (f. 64v), and 'buscan le que se auía de huyr' for 'buscan lo que . . .' (f. 79r). And sometimes the context will cause difficulty in the correction of what would otherwise be an obvious error, such as 'bramauan' for 'brumauan' (f. 17v of the first edition, and five other editions of 1626). Or unfamiliarity with Latin will prevent the correction of something like 'tetegit' for 'tetigit' (f. 17r of the first edition, and five other editions of 1626).

would change the date of the titlepage of his copy to that of the previous year. Such a change would probably not represent an unconscious slip, and we would have to say that the copyist made the change knowing in advance that it would produce an anomaly: a MS whose form was that of a printed edition, but whose final date (that of the titlepage) antedated the dates of the preliminaries.[19] It seems to me much more reasonable to believe that the copyist made no changes: that he dated the titlepage of the MS in 1625 because that date appeared on the titlepage of the text which he was copying. Since every copyist works with a certain mechanical regularity induced by the mental repetition of each phrase twice, it is very possible that on copying a text whose dates were those which appear in the MS, the anomaly would escape him. In addition, the first and most normal instinct would be to reproduce with more or less accuracy the text which he had before him.

The date on the titlepage of the MS might suggest that the source of its text was a printed edition dated 1625. It does not seem likely, however, that such an edition ever existed (see Chap. II, A). And even if its existence were a fact, it is certain that any edition dated 1625 would have had a different set of preliminaries from those which appear, dated 1626, in the MS and the known editions (no printer would have dared to publish an edition whose official preliminaries were dated in the future). This means that the source of the preliminaries of the MS must have been an edition dated 1626, and therefore any theory that the MS was copied in part from an edition of 1625 would have to rest upon the unlikely assumption that the scribe created an

[19] Since in the seventeenth century the *aprobaciones* and *licencias* of a book were written out and dated before the final printing of the complete volume, there exist many books whose preliminaries are dated a year earlier than the titlepage (the best known example is the *Quijote* of 1605; the preliminaries of Quevedo's *Todas las obras en prosa,* Madrid, 1650, date from 1644, 1648, and 1650—see Astrana, *Verso,* p. 1391). It is clear that printers were careful to place on the titlepage the date of the current year; in view of the censorship in effect in the seventeenth century, I doubt that any printer would have dared to print on the titlepage of a book a date which might seem to be a patent falsification.

intentional conflation composed of the titlepage and text of one edition, and the preliminaries of another, later edition. Furthermore, the texts of the MS and the first edition may perhaps be too closely related to permit the intervention of another printed edition.

As mentioned above, the last line of the titlepage of the first edition is lacking in the MS ("A costa de Roberto Duport, Mercader de Libros"). There also appears in the edition the following short *licencia,* which is missing in the MS: "Yo he visto este libro, y no hallo cosa en él por la qual no se deua imprimir, y assí le doy licencia para hazerlo, en Zaragoça, a 23 de hebrero de 1626. [signed:] Mendoza, Assessor." It is clear that the scribe of the MS did not omit this *licencia* for lack of space: the last half of the page which would have carried it is completely blank in the MS. And since the scribe copied all of the other preliminaries, it is difficult to understand why he would omit this *licencia,* had he seen it. Once more, it seems to me that in this case the scribe did not copy something simply because it was not in the text from which he worked. In other words, as suggested by the numerous errors found in the first edition, and the date on its titlepage, the MS was probably not copied from that edition.

D. CONCLUSION

Much of the evidence discussed in this chapter indicates that while the texts of the MS and the first edition are closely related, neither is the direct source of the other.

As mentioned in section A, the titlepages and preliminaries of the MS and the first edition are nearly identical, as are several significant omissions and errors shared by both texts, but not found in any other known editions. This close similarity suggests that if neither text is the source of the other, then both may have been derived from a single source.

If the MS and the first edition were both copied from a single source, but independently of each other, the problem of explaining the puzzlingly high percentage of corrected errors would not exist, for neither text would have been subject to the unique errors in the other. The single source would have contained the twenty-five manifest errors shared by the MS and the first edition, together with the passage omitted by haplography in the MS, and the five errors which the scribe of the MS corrected with palimpsest readings. Since the MS contains neither the last line of the titlepage of the edition ("A costa de Roberto Duport, Mercader de Libros"), nor the short *licencia* dated February 23, 1626, it is most probable that the source also lacked these items, at least when the MS was made (both may well have been inserted while the first edition was being printed). It is further probable that the date on the titlepage of the source was 1625, which the scribe of the MS copied mechanically, but which the printer of the edition changed to 1626 when he set up the titlepage in that year (as explained above in note 19, this was the usual procedure). Since the source was submitted to the censors in January, 1626 (the *aprobación* and the *licencias* are all dated in January and February of 1626), it is quite logical to suppose that its text was compiled as early as 1625, with a titlepage naturally dated that year.

The fact that the MS contains the *licencia* dated February 11, 1626, but not the one dated February 23, 1626, may perhaps indicate that it was made during the interval between these two dates, and before the printing of the first edition. In addition it is likely that the manuscript copy from which type was set for the first edition would have been destroyed after the edition had been printed.

In conclusion, although the Frías MS was copied from the same source as the first edition, its text is slightly earlier and considerably purer than that of the edition.

II

THE EARLY VERSION IN SEVEN
EDITIONS DATED 1626

A. THE *POLÍTICA* NOT PUBLISHED IN 1625

A TRADITION, which may or may not be reliable, states that the *Política de Dios* was published in Zaragoza in 1625. The first reference to such an edition appears in a manuscript bibliography of Spanish books compiled by the seventeenth-century scholar Tomás Tamayo de Vargas. Nicolás Antonio, who, we know, had seen Tamayo's bibliography, repeats the date 1625, and so does Pascual Bueno, stating that his information had been obtained from Nicolás Antonio.[1] Tamayo de Vargas is thus the only real authority for the supposition that the *Política* was printed in 1625.

No bibliographer has ever claimed to have seen an edition of the *Política* dated 1625—not even the assiduous Manuel Jiménez Catalán, who made a special study of printing in Zaragoza in the seventeenth century.[2] The existence of such an

---

[1] Tomás Tamayo de Vargas, "Junta de libros, la mayor que España ha visto en su lengua, hasta el año de MDCXXIV," Biblioteca Nacional de Madrid, MS 9752, pp. 199-200. I am very much indebted to my good friend Don José Antonio Martínez Bara, Conservador de la Sección de Consejos, of the Archivo Histórico Nacional, Madrid, for these references to Tamayo de Vargas, and for the information that the "Junta de libros," although evidently dated 1624, contains references to books published as late as 1627, such as "Emanuel Luciro, *Felipe IV*, Amberes, 1627." Nicolás Antonio, *Bibliotheca Hispana Nova* (Madrid, 1788; first ed. Rome, 1672), s.v. Franciscus de Quevedo Villegas (on the date 1625), and s.v. Thomas Tamayo de Vargas (on Antonio's use of Tamayo's bibliography, which was then in the Barberini Library). Pascual Bueno, ed. *Providencia de Dios,* by Quevedo (Zaragoza, 1700), "Catálogo de las obras de . . . Quevedo," f. [8r] on the date 1625, and f. [6r] on Bueno's use of Nicolás Antonio.

[2] *Ensayo de una tipografía zaragozana del siglo XVII* (Zaragoza, 1927), pp. 150-154.

Polytica de Dios. Govierno de
Christo, y Tyrania de Satanas.

Escriuelo con las plumas delos Euangelistas Don francisco de queuedo villegas, Cauallero del orden de Santiago, y señor dela villa de Juan
Abad.

Al Exmo Conde Duque, gran canciller
mi señor, Don Gaspar de Gusman, conde de Oliuares, Sumiller de corps.
y cauallerizo mayor desu Magestad.

Con licencia.
En Zaragoza por Pedro Verges a los señales.
año. 1 6 2 5.

Frías Manuscript. Author's collection

POLITICA DE DIOS.

GOVIERNO DE CHRISTO:
TYRANIA DE SATANAS.

Eſcriuelo con las plumas de los Euangeliſtas, Don Fran-
ciſco de Queuedo Villegas, Cauallero del Orden de
Santiago, y ſeñor de la Villa de Iuan Abad.

Al Conde Duque, gran Canciller, mi ſeñor, Don
Gaſpar de Guzman, Conde de Oliuares,
Sumilier de Corps, y Cauallerizo
mayor de ſu Mageſtad.

CON LICENCIA.

En Zaragoça: Por Pedro Verges: A los Señales.
Año M. DC. XXVI.
A coſta de Roberto Duport, Mercader de Libros.

First Zaragoza Edition (X). Biblioteca Nacional de Lisboa

POLITICA DE DIOS.

GOVIERNO
DE CHRISTO:
TYRANIA DE SATANAS.

17— 6

Eſcriuelo con las plumas de los Euangeliſtas, Don Fran-
ciſco de Queuedo Villegas, Cauallero del Orden de
Santiago, y ſeñor de la Villa de Iuan Abad.

Al Conde Duque, gran Canciller, mi ſeñor, Don
Gaſpar de Guzman, Conde de Oliuares,
Sumilier de Corps, y Cauallerizo
mayor de ſu Mageſtad.

CON LICENCIA.

En Zaragoça: Por Pedro Verges: A los Señales.
Año M. DC. XXVI.
A coſta de Roberto Duport, Mercader de Libros.

POLITICA
DE DIOS,

GOVIERNO DE CHRISTO;
TIRANIA DE
SATANAS.

ESCRIVELO CON LAS PLV-
mas de los Evangelistas , Don Francisco de Que-
vedo Villegas , Cavallero del Orden de
Santiago , y Señor de la Villa de
Iuan Abad.

AL CONDE DVQVE, GRAN
Canciller; mi señor, Don Gaspar de Guzman, Conde de Olivares, Sumiller de
Corps, y Cavallerizo Mayor de
su Magestad.

CON LICENCIA,

En Zaragoça; Por Pedro Verges; a los Señales.
Año M. DC. XXVI.

Acosta de Roberto Duport, Mercader de libros.

Third Zaragoza Edition (Z). Boston Public Library

POLITICA DE
DIOS. GOVIERNO DE CHRISTO.

AVTOR DON FRANCISCO DE Queuedo Villegas, Cauallero de la Orden de Santiago, señor de la villa de la Torre de Iuan Abad.

A DON GASPAR DE GVZMAN
Conde Duque, gran Canciller
mi señor.

LLEVA AÑADIDOS TRES CAPITVLOS que le faltauan, y algunas planas, y renglones, y va restituido a la verdad de su original.

Paul. 1. Cor. 3. *Vnusquisque autem videat quomodo super adificet, fundamentum enim aliud nemo potest ponere prater id quod positum est, quod est* CHRISTVS IESVS.

Ioan. capit. 13. *Exemplum enim dedi vobis, vt quemadmodum ego sen vobis, ita & vos faciatis.*

Año   ❀   1626
CON PRIVILEGIO

En Madrid, Por la viuda de Alonso Martin.
A costa de Alonso Perez mercader de libros.

First Authorized Edition (Q). Biblioteca Nacional de Madrid

FERIA DE DIOS. GOVIERNO DE CHRISTO.

AVTOR DON FRANCISCO DE Queuedo Villegas, Cauallero de la Orden de Santiago, señor de la villa de la Torre de Iuan Abad.

A DON GASPAR DE GVZMAN Conde Duque, gran Canciller mi señor.

LLEVA AÑADIDOS TRES CAPITVLOS que le faltauan, y algunas plazas, y renglones, y va restituido a la verdad de su original.

Paulo 1.Cor.3. Vnusquisque autē videat quomodo super ædificet, fundamentum enim aliud nemo potest ponere præter id quod positum est, quod est. CHRISTVS IESVS.

Ioan.cap.13. Exemplum enim dedi vobis, vt quemadmodum ego feci vobis, ita & vos faciatis.

Año 1626.

CON PRIVILEGIO.

En Madrid, Por la viuda de Alonso Martin.
A costa de Alonso Perez mercader de libros.

Second Authorized Edition (R). Biblioteca Nacional de Lisboa

En el govierno superior de Dios sigue al entendimiento la voluntad.

VIendo Dios, en los primeros passos que dio el tiempo, tan achacoso el Imperio de Adam tan introduzida la lisonja del demonio; y tan poderosa con la persuasion contra el precepto; y recien nacido el mundo, tan crecida la embidia en los primeros herma-nos, que a su diligencia debio la primera man-cha de sangre; el desconocimiento con tanta fuerça, que oso escalar el Cielo; y vltimamen-te aduirtiendo quan mal se gouernauan los hombres por si, y que vnos de otros no podiã aprender fino doctrina defectuosa, y mal en-tendida, y acreditada por la vanidad de los dessosos porque no viuiessen en desconcerta-da tirania, debaxo del imperio del hombre, las demas criaturas, y consigo los hombres; de-terminò de baxar en vna de las personas a go-uernar el mundo, y a enseñar (bien a su costa, y mas de los que no le supieren, o quisieren imitar) la politica de la verdad, y de la vida. No vino en la persona del Padre, ni en la del Espíritu; baxó en la del Hijo, que es el enten-dimiento, y fue embiado por Legislador al mun-

y tirania de sus amos.

mundo, por su padre, Christo. Despues le si-
guio el Espiritulanto, que es el Amor y voluntad.

El entendimiento guia a la voluntad si le sigue. La voluntad arrastra al entendimiento quando le haze lugar.

El entendimiento es la vista de la volun-tad, y si no preceden sus decretos en toda o-bra, a tiethro; y a escuras caminan las potencias del alma.

Asperamente reprehende Christo este mo-do de hablar, valiendose imperiosamente de la voluntad; quando le dixeron, *Volumus à te signum videre.* Queremos que hagas vn mila-gro; y en otra parte *Volumus, ut quodcunque petierimus facias nobis.* Los hijos del Zebedeo, Queremos que nos concedas todo lo que te pidieremos; y en otros muchos lugares no quiere Christo, que la voluntad propria se entremeta en sus obras, condena por descor-tes este modo de hablar. Y vltimamente enfe-ñando a los hombres el lenguage que han de tener con su Padre, que esta en el Cielo; Lo primero, les haze resignar la voluntad, y orde-na que digamos en la oracion del Padre nue-stro, fiat voluntas tua, hagase tu voluntad, pur-
que:

First Zaragoza Edition (X)

Politica de Dios, govierno de Chriſto,

En el govierno ſuperior de Dios ſigue al entendi-
miento la voluntad.

VIendo Dios en los primeros paſſos que
dio el tiempo tan achacoſo el Imperio
de Adam, tan introducida la liſonja del demonio, y tan poderoſa con el, la perſuaſion contra el precepto, y recien nacido el mundo,
tan crecida la inuidia en los primeros herma-
nos, que a ſu diligencia deuo la primera man-
cha de ſangre, el deſconocimiento con tantas
fuerças, que oſo eſcalar el Cielo, y vltimamen-
te aduirtiendo quan malſe gouernaſſan los
hombres por ſi, y que vnos ſe otros no podiã
aprender ſino doctrina defectuoſa, y mal en-
tendida, y acreditada, por la vanidad de los
deſſeos, porque no viuieſſen en deſconcerta-
da tirania debaxo del imperio del hombre
las demas criaturas, y conſigo los hombres, de
terminó de baxar en vna delas perſonas a go-
uernar el mundo, y a enſeñar (biena ſu coſta,
y mas de los que no ſeſupieren, o quiſieren
imitar) la politica de la verdad, y de la vida.
No vino en la perſona del Padre, ni en la del
Eſpiritu: baxó en la del Hijo, que es el entendimiento, y fue embiado por legiſlador al
mun-

mundo por ſu padre, Chriſto. Deſpues le ſi-
guió el Eſpiritulanto, que es el Amor y voluntad.

El entendimiento guia a la voluntad ſi le
ſigue. La voluntad arraſtra al entendimiento, ro
quando le haze lugar.

El entendimiento es la viſta de la voluntad, y ſi no preceden ſus decretos en toda o-
bra, a tiento y a eſcuras caminan las potencias
del alma.

Aſperamente reprehende Chriſto eſte modo de hablar, valiendoſe imperioſamente de
la voluntad, quando le dixeron, *Volumus à te*
ſignum videre. Queremos que hagas vn mila-
gro; en otra parte, *Volumus, vt quodcumq; pe-*
tierimus facias nobis. Los hijos del Zebedeo:
Queremos que nos concedas todo lo que te
pidieremos, y en otros muchos lugares no
quiere Chriſto, que la voluntad propria ſe
entremeta en ſus obras, condena por deſcor-
tes eſte modo de hablar. Y vltimamente enſe-
ñando a los hombres el lenguage que han de
tener con ſu Padre, que eſta en el Cielo. Lo
primero les haze reſignar la voluntad, y orde-
na que digamos en la oracion del Padre nue-
ſtro, *fiat voluntas tua,* hagaſe tu voluntad, porque

Second Zaragoza Edition (Y)

edition was denied by Aureliano Fernández-Guerra in 1852 and again, with Menéndez y Pelayo, in 1897, on the grounds that Tamayo de Vargas was confusing the date on the titlepage of the Frías MS (1625) with the date of a known Zaragoza edition (1626).[3] Provided that Tamayo knew the Frías MS, this explanation is not implausible (Tamayo's accuracy is not above question).

Whether or not Tamayo ever did see the MS, there is a certain amount of bibliographical and historical evidence to the effect that the *Política* was not published in 1625. The preliminaries in the known Zaragoza editions are all dated in 1626, which means that any edition published in 1625 would have had different preliminaries (under the censorship then in effect in Spain, no bookseller could possibly have published a book whose official *aprobaciones* and *licencia* were dated in a future year). And since the original set of preliminaries was almost always used in successive editions,[4] it is highly probable that any preliminaries written in 1625 would have reappeared in the 1626 editions. None do so appear. Even more significant is the fact that the MS, dated 1625, has an *aprobación* dated 1626, which is some indication that no earlier *aprobación* was available.

What historical evidence we have is circumstantial, and rests on the knowledge that in 1626 Quevedo accompanied King Philip IV on a state journey to convene regional parliaments in Aragon, Valencia and Catalonia.[5] The royal party, which on this journey was relatively small and travelled without undue delay, left Madrid on January 7, 1626, proceeding directly to Zaragoza. Although there is no record of Quevedo's activities in Zaragoza,

[3] Fernández-Guerra, ed. *Obras de Quevedo,* in *BAE* XXIII (Madrid, 1852), p. xcii, col a, no. 2 ("Catálogo de ediciones"), and p. 3 ("Advertencia del colector"). Fernández-Guerra and Menéndez y Pelayo, eds. *Obras completas de Quevedo* (Seville, 1897), I, 408, no. 2 ("Catálogo de ediciones").

[4] See, for example, the persistent reprinting of the preliminaries of the 1626 Zaragoza editions, documented below in Appendix II.

[5] Fernández-Guerra and Menéndez y Pelayo, "Vida de Quevedo," in *Obras completas de Quevedo* (Seville, 1897), I, 115 (Bibliófilos Andaluces).

he probably arrived there on January 13, 1626, and would have remained a week until Philip moved on. [6]

It is perhaps significant that the first *aprobación* for the 1626 edition of the *Política* was signed in Zaragoza within a few weeks of Quevedo's arrival, or on January 26. This edition was printed late in February, 1626, by Pedro Verges, for the bookseller Roberto Duport. It seems likely that either Verges or Duport had some connection with Quevedo himself: in the spring of 1626, they published more editions of the *Política*, and the first edition of the *Buscón;* in 1627 they published the first edition of Quevedo's *Desvelos soñolientos,* a version of the *Sueños* corrected and certified by Quevedo's personal friend Lorenzo Vander Hammen.[7]

Although Duport implied that he was publishing the *Política*

---

[6] On the date of departure from Madrid, see Gonzalo de Céspedes y Meneses, *Primera parte de la historia de D. Felippe IIII, rey de las Españas* (Lisbon, 1631), lib. VII, cap. i, p. 550a. On this page Céspedes refers to the date of departure as "a 7 del mes," but the month in question is identified as January on p. 548a. On the small size of the royal party and its relatively rapid itinerary, he says that Philip left Madrid "con poca gente de su guarda, y menos séguito [sic] de señores," and that they travelled "a la lijera y aorrado" (p. 550a). The date of arrival in Zaragoza appears in Diego Dormer, "Anales de Aragon," Academia de la Historia, Col. Salazar, MS G-43, f. 204r. Philip arrived in Barbastro, the next stop, on Jan. 20 (Dormer, f. 209r). Martin Hume's statement in *The Court of Philip IV* (London, 1907), p. 163, that the royal party left Madrid for Zaragoza on Sept. 7, 1625, is surely a mistake: in addition to Céspedes y Meneses, the date of January 7, 1626, is attested by two other contemporary historians: Matías de Novoa, *Historia de Felipe IV,* in *Colección de documentos inéditos para la historia de España* (Madrid, 1878), LXIX, 15, and Andrés de Almansa y Mendoza, *Cartas,* in *Colección de libros españoles raros o curiosos* (Madrid, 1886), XVII, 321.

[7] The editions of the *Buscón* and the *Sueños* are described in Luis Astrana Marín, *Obras completas: obras en verso,* by Quevedo (Madrid, 1943), pp. 1375-76, "Catálogo de ediciones." Vander Hammen's role in the preparation of the *Desvelos soñolientos* is apparent in his letter to Francisco Jiménez de Urrea (also a friend of Quevedo), originally printed on f. [4r] of the *Desvelos* edition, and now available in Luis Astrana Marín, *Obras completas en prosa* (Madrid, 1945), p. 1696. Astrana's two editions are hereinafter referred to as *Verso* and *Prosa* respectively.

without Quevedo's consent, his statement is so curious that it deserves to be quoted in full:

El librero al lector

Por auerme pedido muchas vezes de Francia y de Italia, y de diferentes partes de España con instancia qualesquier obras de don Francisco de Queuedo Villegas, y auiendo entendido esta *Política de Dios* andaua manuscripta con grande estimación, y sabiendo que en la lengua francesa y la italiana estaua traduzida, hize diligencia hasta que tuue vna copia, que es la que doy a la estampa, con desseo de que se conozca quanto sabe bolar aquella pluma, que ya con la cultura, ya con la gracia y agudeza, ha admirado y suspendido por muchos años todas las naciones. Puede ser en partes salga defectuosa la impressión; desto será causa no yr reconocida de su autor, que en tanta humildad detiene estudios tan grandes.

Roberto Duport[8]

Much of what Duport says in this exaggerated and evasive statement is questionable. There is no evidence that the *Política* had been translated into any foreign language before 1626, nor is there any to the effect that it had circulated widely in MS form "con grande estimación." And if any foreigners had asked for copies of Quevedo's works, they would probably have been interested in the *Sueños* and the *Buscón,* for there is abundant evidence that MSS of these satires had circulated very widely (see below, Chapter III, n. 9). The exaggerations and the highly flattering tone of the entire paragraph, and especially of the last sentence, with its improbable reference to humility, are characteristic of the dedications which seventeenth-century printers wrote for their patrons, or for people to whom they owed great favors. Had Duport received from a writer of Quevedo's reputation a MS of the *Política,* and perhaps another of the *Buscón,* he would certainly have been inclined to express his gratitude. (This might not have been the case if, as implied in his statement, Duport had searched for and found such MSS on his own initiative.) And it is entirely possible that Quevedo would have

[8] *Política de Dios,* first ed. (Zaragoza, 1626), f. [4r]. Reprinted in Astrana, *Prosa,* p. 377, n. 1. Italics mine.

preferred to avoid the difficulties he had once had with book censors, by finding a publisher outside the realm of Castille, and by dissociating himself from the publication of the book.[9]

In short, I believe that the available evidence supports the conclusion that the *Política* was not published in Zaragoza in 1625.

B. THREE SEPARATE EDITIONS PRINTED IN ZARAGOZA

1. BIBLIOGRAPHY

In attempting to establish the filiation of the 1626 editions of the *Política de Dios,* I first compared the text of the Harvard University copy, dated Zaragoza, 1626, with the texts of the editions published in the same year in other cities. The results obtained were unfortunately as clear as they were contradictory, and I was persuaded that the solution to the problem might lie in a close examination of all of the known copies of the Zaragoza edition.

This edition was first described in 1852 by Aureliano Fernández-Guerra, who had seen a copy then owned by Francisco González de Vera. Fernández-Guerra's description includes a transcription of the titlepage and an unpaginated list of the preliminary material, but no collation; his time-worn notes were reprinted by Menéndez y Pelayo in 1897, and again by Luis Astrana Marín in 1932.[10]

---

[9] In 1610 Quevedo prepared a MS of one or more of the *Sueños* for publication, but the censor refused to approve the text (*Prosa,* p. 183). With the exception of the irreproachable *Epítome a la historia de la vida exemplar . . . del bienaventurado F. Tomás de Villanueva* (Madrid, 1620), Quevedo apparently published no full-length book until the appearance of the *Política.* He claimed, when he published the revised version of the *Política* (Madrid, 1626), that the Zaragoza edition, to which he did not assign a date, had been printed "sin mi assistencia y sabiduría, falto de capítulos y planas, defectuoso y adulterado" (Madrid ed., f. [16v]; *Prosa,* preliminaries, p. 377a-b). But this declaration, as its context shows, was prompted by a desire to disown an edition which had been severely criticized by Quevedo's enemies.

[10] Fernández-Guerra, *BAE* XXIII, p. xcii; Menéndez y Pelayo, ed.

I do not know the present location of the copy Fernández-Guerra used (it is doubtful that Menéndez y Pelayo ever saw it). Astrana Marín mentions one copy now in the Biblioteca Nacional de Madrid, but there are at least ten others in existence, all dated Zaragoza, 1626. These eleven copies, however, do not all share identical textual and typographical characteristics.

Three of the eleven copies, now located severally in the Biblioteca Universitaria de Sevilla, Biblioteca Nacional de Lisboa, and Biblioteca da Ajuda (Lisbon), are identical in foliation, and in textual and typographical characteristics (there is not even any variation in the punctuation, or the division of the text into pages and lines, or the positioning of catchwords and signature marks). Finally, the use of McKerrow's ruler test[11] shows that the spacing of the letters in each line of print is identical, something which would be almost impossible in two different editions published in the seventeenth century. The edition which these three copies represent will hereinafter be referred to as edition X.

Six more copies may be found in the University of Illinois

Obras completas (Seville, 1897), I, 408; Astrana, *Verso,* pp. 1373-1374. I have been unable to identify Francisco González de Vera. There is a detailed but not very accurate description of the University of Zaragoza copy of the *Política* (Zaragoza, 1626), in Manuel Jiménez Catalán, *Ensayo de una tipografía zaragozana del siglo XVII* (Zaragoza, 1927), pp. 153-154, and another description of a different edition (also Zaragoza, 1626), in Antonio Palau y Dulcet, *Manual del librero hispanoamericano* (Barcelona, 1923), VI, 191. All of these bibliographers mistakenly believed that they were describing the first edition of the *Política.*

[11] "There is one other test that we may try. I have used it several times and never known it fail to give a clear answer one way or the other. It is this: Take any page of the book and find in it two full stops at a distance of some ten or a dozen lines apart. . . . Lay a ruler on the page from one of these stops to the other and note the letters or parts of letters that it cuts. If a rule placed in a similar position in the other copy cuts the same letters, the chances are many hundreds to one that the two pages were printed from the same setting-up of type; for however carefully a compositor followed his original, the irregularity in the casting of type and spaces would almost inevitably prevent the two prints corresponding in this respect." Ronald B. McKerrow, *An Introduction to Bibliography* (Oxford, 1949) p. 183.

Library, Biblioteca Universitaria de Zaragoza, Biblioteca Nacional de Madrid, Biblioteca Casanatense (Rome), Bibliothèque de l'Arsenal (Paris), and Bibliothèque Mazarine (Paris). With the exception of five errors in foliation, all of these copies share identical textual and typographical characteristics. Although one error in foliation is common to all copies (folio 26 is numbered as 20), five more errors are distributed as follows: f. 51 is numbered as 50 and f. 53 as 52 (Illinois, Mazarine, Arsenal and Zaragoza), f. 69 as 6 (Madrid and Zaragoza), f. 74 as 7 (Illinois and Casanatense), and f. 81 as 8 (Illinois, Casanatense, Mazarine and Madrid).

It should be noted that folios 51-53, 69, 74 and 81 are found in four different signatures: H, K, L and M. This means that the puzzling distribution of the errors among the six copies of the edition is merely a reflection of two practices usual in seventeenth-century printing. First, in order to save type, the different signatures of a book would be printed separately, with the forms broken up after each signature had been run off, and the same type reset for the next signature. The printed signatures were later bound together into a book, but not necessarily in the order in which they actually came off the press. Secondly, printers often made changes as a signature was coming off the press (if an error was discovered in one of the first sheets run off, the press could be stopped, the erroneous character corrected in the type, and the remaining sheets run off with the correction). Thus it is not surprising that various copies of one and the same edition should display different combinations of errors in different signatures.[12]

The uniformity of all of the textual and typographical char-

---

[12] Although there is no instance in the early editions of the *Política,* it is of course possible to have disagreement within a signature. Each signature was printed first on one side of the paper, and then on the other. Corrections could be made during the printing of the first side, the sheets then turned over, and run back through the press for the printing of the second side. But they would not necessarily be run back in the order in which they were first printed, and more corrections might be made during the printing of the second side.

acteristics of the six copies under discussion is therefore not disturbed by the distribution of the errors in foliation, and it may be said that these copies form a single edition, hereinafter referred to as edition Y.

Although editions X and Y present the same text on their titlepages, the same foliation, and roughly the same division of the corpus of the text into signatures and pages, there are considerable differences between the two. In the first place, there are many variant readings in the text, six of which involve the insertion into Y of passages between four and thirteen words in length, which do not appear at all in X.[13] Secondly, the extensive application of McKerrow's ruler test to numerous folios shows that the spacing between the letters in the lines of print varies a great deal. This is true even when there are no textual variants, and when the justification of the right-hand margins is identical (see plate of f. 3r; note also that many letters which in edition X are placed under certain others of the next line above, are not so placed in edition Y). Further differences between X and Y occur in the positioning of catchwords, signature marks and running headings. Finally, the division of the text into lines differs, and this appears clearly in the justification of the right-hand margins of many folios. On f. 28r, for instance, in a paragraph in which there are no textual variants to disturb the margin, the right-hand margin of X reads as follows (lines 12-19): "sama/y q res/consulta./māde/consuma a/reprehẽsiō:/hōbre/ saluallas. [space]/." In Y the margin of the same lines reads as follows: "sa-/y q/consul-/mā/cōsuma/reprehen/hō/saluallas [no period and no space]/."[14]

It is inconceivable that two printed texts with differences of such varied kinds could represent anything less than two separate editions made from different forms.

There exist two more copies of the *Política* dated Zaragoza, 1626, one located in the Ticknor Collection of the Boston Public

---

[13] The six variants referred to are quoted in full on pages 9-10.
[14] Further good examples on ff. 4r, 24v, 39r, 62v, 63r, etc.

Library, and the other in the Harvard University Law Library.[15] These two copies represent a single edition (abbrev. Z), and this edition shares with X and Y the same *aprobaciones* and *licencias,* the same division of the text into signatures, and roughly the same division into folios (Z contains 77 numbered folios rather than 81 as in X and Y, simply because in Z the numbering begins four folios after that of X and Y). But as may be seen in the bibliographical description in Appendix II, the titlepage of Z differs considerably from X and Y in punctuation, capitalization, and division into lines; further differences in the text itself include the numbering of the folios (mentioned above), the lack of any errors in the foliation of Z, the division of the text into lines, and finally numerous variants and errors (112 unique errors in forty per cent of the text of Z—see below).

In conclusion, it can be said that in 1626 the *Política de Dios* was printed in Zaragoza not once, but three times.

2. Textual Criticism

It is clear from the foregoing bibliographical discussion that editions X and Y are so closely related that one was almost certainly copied from the other. While the bibliographical characteristics of Z are not so similar to X or Y as these are to each other, it is nevertheless most probable that Z was made from an edition very close to X and Y.

In analyzing X and Y, it is perhaps best to take up first a few more or less lengthy passages which appear in one or the other of the two editions, but not in both (this type of omission or insertion often furnishes clear proof of filiation).

The two longest of these passages appear in edition Y, but not in X. They read as follows (the words missing in X are in square brackets):

> En el libro del Talmud Berachot, que quiere dezir 'De las védiciones,' capítulo 'Hen Vndin,' ['No estarán,' dice Rabbi

---

[15] On the blank leaf opposite the titlepage of the Ticknor copy there is a MS note in English which contains several erroneous statements about the edition, including the confusion of the pirated edition of the *Buscón* with the authorized edition of the *Política.*

Eliazar, 'desde el día que el Templo se destruyó;'] dize el Hebreo 'Sarei Tefilo,' 'Las puertas de la oración se cerraron' (editions X and Y, f. 7v; Astrana, *Prosa,* chapter ii, p. 382a, but with this passage omitted).

Christo . . . ya los auía dicho que conuenía que cada vno tomasse su cruz, y le siguiesse, . . . pero esto del padecer, y del morir, quiere que sea quando en su ausencia y en su lugar gouiernen; aora son súbditos, padezca el Maestro y la caueça; [quando temporalmente le succedieron (*sic*) y cada vno assistió (*sic*) el gouierno de su prouincia,] quien aquí, siendo obejas, los desuía la mala palabra, el empellón, la cuerda y la cárcel, quando sean pastores, los embiará el cuchillo, el fuego, las piedras (X, Y, f. 39v; *Prosa* x, p. 399a).[16]

Although it can be said that the length and complexity of these passages indicate that they were not the inventions of a compositor, it is doubtful that they furnish reliable information about the filiation of editions X and Y. The first passage seems designed to convey additional information, but its presence by no means clarifies the meaning of the sentence as a whole, for it creates awkward transitions. The second passage seems intended to clarify the contrast between the time when Christ was with the apostles on earth, and the time after His ascension when the apostles were alone on earth (each period is distinguished by one of two contrasting attitudes towards the apostles). Apart from the confusing and almost erroneous use of the preterite tense in 'succedieron' and 'assistió' (possibly due to the failure of the person who may have inserted these words to appreciate the use of the historical present tense in the rest of the passage), it seems to me that the words in question do not clarify the text much because it is already quite clear without them: the author has already referred twice to the time described in the insertion, if such it was ("quando en su ausencia y en su lugar gouiernen," and "quando sean pastores"), and he has clarified the temporal difference each time ("aora son . . ." and "quien aquí . . .").

Whatever our theories or opinions on these details, it is clear that neither the omission nor the insertion of the passages can

---

[16] As explained in Chapter I, n. 4, I have modernized the capitalization, accentuation, and, cautiously, the punctuation of the original texts.

be proved a manifest error, and that they do not furnish really clear evidence on which to establish the filiation of editions X and Y. If, for instance, Y was made from X, it would be difficult to say whether these passages were inserted to restore lacunae in X, or merely as after-thoughts to elaborate or "improve" on X. If on the other hand X was copied from Y, the passages could have been omitted either by design or by accident. Even the plausible conclusion that these passages are not obvious omissions does little to prove that they are insertions.

Two of the five remaining passages which appear in Y but not in X present much the same sort of problem as those discussed above.[17] In the third and fourth of the five passages, Y presents a corrupt text, indicating that X may have been the earlier edition.[18] But in the fifth passage there is evidence to the contrary: the reading of X, though not really corrupt, is less correct than that of Y.[19] Thus the series of passages missing from

---

[17] "Quando el Rey Christo Iesvs en este Euangelio enseña, como verdad, vida y camino a todos los monarcas el méthodo de la justicia real, ¿quién más en desgracia de Dios que el Demonio? [¿Que vna legión de ellos?] Criatura desconocida, vassallo aleuoso, que se amotinó contra Dios" (X, Y, f. 14r; *Prosa* iii, p. 385a). "En los malos, en los impíos se ha de mostrar la misericordia, por los delinquentes se han de hazer fineças. [¿Quién padeció por el bueno?] Con estas palabras habló elegantemente la caridad del apóstol San Pablo, Rom. 5: 'Vt quid enim Christus . . .' " (X, Y, f. 15v; *Prosa* iii, p. 386a).

[18] In these two passages, the corruptions introduced by Y can best be exposed by copying out each text in full. In the first of the two, X reads as follows (punctuation as in the original): "Siendo rey pobre, y de mejor mundo, en éste fue rey de todos, por quien era, y porque lo dexaua. De pocos que le conocieron, escogió doze hombres, vno le vendió, otro le negó, los más le huyeron, algunos le dudaron" (X, f. 8v; *Prosa* ii, p. 382a). Y reads as follows (punctuation as in the original): "Siendo rey pobre, y de mejor mundo, en éste fue rey de todos, por quien era, y porque lo dexaua de pocos que le conocieran, y entre doze hombres, no cabal el número, que vno le vendió, otro le negó, los más le huyeron, algunos le dudaron" (Y, f. 8v). In the second passage, the Latin phrase "Et venit [Y: veniunt] Iesus Ierosolyman, et cum introisset in templum" (Mark xi.15; cf. Math. xxi.12, John ii.13-14), is translated in X as "Y vino Iesús a Ierusalém, y como entrasse en el templo" (X, f. 62v; *Prosa* xix, p. 416b), but in Y as "Y entró Iesús en el templo en Ierusalém, y como entrasse en el templo" (Y, f. 62 v).

[19] In this passage the Latin phrase "Dixit ergo vnus ex discipulis eius,

X do not furnish clear evidence of the filiation of X and Y.

In addition to the passages omitted by X, there are two omitted by Y but present in X. One of these offers the same difficulties as the first two discussed above: it may have been omitted in a second printing in order to avoid tautology (the repetition of the verb 'dar'), or it may have been inserted in a second printing in order to insure the clarity of the sentence.[20] In the other passage, the omission of the words in question may not constitute a manifest error, but it alters and obscures the meaning to such an extent that it is probable that the passage originally contained the missing words.[21]

As in the case of the passages missing from edition X, those missing from Y do not furnish evidence sufficiently clear and reliable to establish the filiation of the two editions. It is thus necessary to examine other types of evidence.

The manifest errors found in editions X and Y may be tabu-

Iudas Iscariotes, qui erat eum traditurus" (John xii.4), is translated as follows (the words missing in X are in square brackets): "Dixo vno de sus dicípulos, Iudas [Iudas varón de Carioth,] que le auía de vender" (X, Y, f. 19v; *Prosa* v, p. 388a).

[20] In this passage, Quevedo summarizes and interprets III Kings, xxii.24, as follows (the words missing in Y are in square brackets): "Llegó oyendo estas razones al profeta Micheas, al varón de Dios, Sedechías, hijo de Caana, y dio vna bofetada en la cara a Micheas. . . . Este Sedechías deuía de ser algún favorecido del Rey . . . ; vio . . . que el desengaño seuero y preuenido le amenaçaua desde los labios del Profeta, y por esso le procuró tapar la boca con la puñada [que le dio], y dar a la verdad tósigo, y veneno en el varón de Dios" (X, Y, ff. 77v-78r; *Prosa* xxiii, p. 424b).

[21] In this passage Quevedo refers to the way in which Christ drove the money-lenders from the temple, and calls upon King Philip to do the same (the words omitted by Y are in square brackets): "Sábese que Vuestra Magestad puede dezir esto por su casa, y porque feruorosamente con su exemplo alienta virtud y valor desembaraçada en sus vassallos; sólo resta que abra los ojos sobre los que la quisieren hazer cueua de ladrones (si alguna insolencia se atreuiere a tanto), y los castigue y alexe de sí; y no será [disculpa dezir que no se atreuerán], antes [Y substitutes 'pero'] temerlo es religión, pues veo que Christo halló en la casa de Dios quien lo hiziesse a sus ojos, y no será más priuilegiada para los atreuimientos de los impíos y codiciosos la casa de algún rey que la casa de Dios" (X, Y, f. 63r; *Prosa* xix, p. 416b-417a).

lated as follows: Unique errors (found in one text alone): X − 41; Y − 79. Common errors (found in both texts): X and Y − 57.[22] It is apparent from these figures that if X had been copied from Y, the compositor of X must have corrected the seventy-nine errors found in the text of Y. But if Y was copied from X, only forty-one errors need have been corrected. Thus on a purely numerical basis it is more likely that X was the source of Y.

This probability is supported by an examination of the types of errors which underwent possible correction. The compositor of an edition, whose hands were occupied with the type and whose eyes were on each individual word or letter rather than on the meaning of entire phrases or sentences, would not find it difficult to discover and correct simple or obvious errors involving orthographical or typographical blunders. To the examples cited in section C of Chapter I, the following may be added (my corrections are in square brackets): "Pregón y amenaça de la sabiiduría [sabiduría]" (X, f. [10v]; *Prosa,* preliminaries, p. 376a). . . . "Las plumas que le siruen de lengnas [lenguas]" (X, f. 2r; *Prosa,* preliminaries, p. 376b). . . . "En otos [otros] muchos lugares" (X, f. 3r; *Prosa* i, p. 379b). . . . "No pensana [pensaua] Iudas" (X, f. 19v; *Prosa* v, p. 388a). . . . "Quien se descuydare ea [en] esta parte" (X, f. 22r; *Prosa* v, p. 389b). . . . "Pidió tan cortesmenie [cortesmente]" (X, f. 48r; *Prosa* xv, p. 409a).

But as mentioned in Chapter I, correction would be far less probable in the case of more subtle and complex errors (my corrections are in square brackets): "Quando le prendieron, milító [limitó] aun las palabras, preso respondió con el silencio" (Y, f. 8v; *Prosa* ii, p. 382a). . . . "Otra vez les dixo, que no sabía [sabían] de que espíritu eran, y los riñó ásperamente, porque se

---

[22] As mentioned above in Chap. I, n. 16, occasional difficulties in distinguishing between variants and errors mean that figures such as those above can only be approximate. But I feel certain that the margin of error is not great. Many of the errors listed above reappear in later editions of the *Política,* but this does not disturb the relationship of X and Y as indicated by these errors. (It would interfere, of course, with an attempt to prove the unity of X and Y, but that is not at issue here.)

enojauan los [con los] que no los seguían" (Y, f. 11r; *Prosa* ii, p. 383b). . . . "Fur erat, et oculos [loculos] habens" (Y, f. 19v; *Prosa* v, p. 388a). . . . "In omnem terram exiuit somnus [sonus] eorum" (Y, f. 44v; *Prosa* xiii, p. 405a, n. 1).

This second group of examples involves readings which would be superficially acceptable to one who was not aware of the syntax or context. Of the seventy-nine unique errors found in edition Y but not in X, some sixty-one are of the type not easily corrected (the second set of examples above is from these errors). But of the forty-one unique errors found in X, about twenty-nine are of the type readily corrected (the first set of examples is drawn from these). Thus it is much more probable that Y corrected twenty-nine easily discovered errors, than that X corrected sixty-one difficult errors.

The theory that edition X is the source of Y is further supported by the punctuation of the two editions: Y contains so many errors in punctuation, including the substitution of commas for colons and question marks, the interruption of sentences by periods and their termination by commas, etc., that it would be most improbable that an edition as correct as X could have been made from Y.[23]

In the text of Z, the remaining edition of the three published in Zaragoza in 1626, there are four more or less lengthy omis-

---

[23] The following are examples of the errors in punctuation in edition Y (in square brackets I insert the punctuation of X): "El les dixo a ellos: 'Qué queréys que haga con vosotros, [?]' y dixeron: 'Concédenos . . .'" (X, Y, f. 43r; *Prosa* xiii, p. 404a). "Qué importa que el rey sea vn ángel, si los ministros son demonios, y entre todos ellos, no halla vn hombre, quien más le ha menester. [?] Qué cosa es vna república, sino vna piscina, [?] qué ha de ser vn rey, sino vn ángel que la mueua, y la dé virtud; [?]" (X, Y, f. 61r; *Prosa* xviii, p. 415b). "Los reyes nacieron para los solos y desamparados, [:] y los entremetidos para peligro y persecución, y carga de los reyes, [;] déstos han de huyr azia aquéllos, [.] quien solicita y pretende el cargo, le engayta, o le compra, o le arrebata [.] quien se contenta con hazerse por la virtud digno del, le merece [.] a estas cosas, no se ha de acudir por relaciones, y por terceros" (X, Y, ff. 61v-62r; *Prosa* xviii, p. 416a). Further examples on ff. 8v, 14r, 15v, 29v, 30r, 41r, 57v, etc.

sions, of which at least two seem to be errors, as follows (I have placed the words missing from Z in square brackets): "Vultis dimitam vobis Regem Iudaeorum? '¿Queréis que dé libertad al Rey de los Iudíos?' Clamaverunt rursus dicentes, Non hunc. Gritaron [otra vez, diciendo, 'No a éste.' Negaron] le la soltura y consintiéronle la dignidad" (Z, f. 2r; Y, f. 6r; *Prosa* ii, p. 381a).
. . . "Ora Patrum (*sic*) tuum in abscondito, [et Pater tuus, qui videt in abscondito], reddet tibi" (Z, f. 75v; Y, f. 80r; *Prosa* xxiv, p. 425b).[24]

The omission in the first example is clearly an error, if only because it forces the Spanish translation "Gritáronle la soltura" to contradict the Latin "Non hunc." In the second example, part of a quotation from Matthew vi. 6 is skipped, with the result that the meaning of what remains is, to say the least, obscured. The fact that both of these passages involve haplography is further evidence that the words in question were omitted by Z rather than inserted by X and Y. Both omissions thus suggest that edition Z was not the source of X or Y.[25]

In analyzing the manifest errors in Z, I have collated a reasonably large portion of the text of the edition, sufficient to furnish clear and consistent conclusions (further collation has confirmed these conclusions).[26] In the particular chapters collated, the er-

[24] My text is taken from Z, with the omitted words as in Y.
[25] The first of the remaining two passages is as follows: "Su caudal luzido de v.m. desempeñó [a los vnos, y satisfizo a los otros con] tanta [Z reads 'tal'] bizarría que parece impossible quede más que dezir de esta materia" (Z, Y, f. [7r]; *Prosa,* letter from Vander Hammen, p. 1684b). In the second passage the text of Z reads: "Quien pidió a Dios conociendo y confessando su misericordia en la petición, ¿ qué no alcançasse?" (Z, f. 40r; *Prosa* xii, p.404b), while Y reads: "Quien pidió a Dios conociendo y confessando en la petición su misericordia, su grandeça, su poder, y su sabiduría, ¿ qué no alcançasse?" (Y, f. 44r).
[26] About forty per cent of the text was collated first: chapters i, ii, iii, iv, x, xx, and all preliminary material. (In the text of the revised Madrid edition of 1626, the only one available in modern editions, these numbers would correspond to chapters ii, iii, iv, v, xiii, xxiv, and such preliminary material as was found in the early editions, including an article which, although numbered chapter i in the revised text, was in the early editions a part of the preliminaries.) Subsequent to the first collation, I analyzed various other chapters from different signatures.

rors in X, Y and Z are as follows: Unique errors: X — 18; Y — 20; Z — 112. Common errors: X and Y — 17; X and Z — none; Y and Z — 28; X, Y and Z — 8. (This last group of eight errors supports the bibliographical evidence discussed above to the effect that all three editions are closely related to each other.)

Since in the portions of the text analyzed, edition Z contains 112 unique errors, or roughly six times as many as X or Y, it is evident that Z is a very corrupt text. The correction of such quantities of errors would be next to impossible, and it is therefore most probable Z was not the source of X or Y.

The fairly close relationship between X, Y and Z suggests the possibility that either X or Y was the source of Z. The fact that Z not only shares with Y the seven passages mentioned on pages 9-10 as missing in X, but in addition lacks the two passages omitted in Y, indicates that Z was made from Y.

This suggestion is confirmed by the distribution of manifest errors in the three editions. As noted above, Y and Z share twenty-eight manifest errors not found in X, while X and Z share none at all which are not also found in Y. If Z had been copied from X, it would be next to impossible to explain not only the twenty-eight errors shared with Y to the exclusion of X, but also the corresponding total absence of any errors shared exclusively by X and Z. On the contrary, this same distribution is convincing evidence that Y was the source of edition Z.

C. FOUR OTHER EDITIONS DATED 1626

1. BIBLIOGRAPHY

The text of the *Política* as found in the three Zaragoza editions was published in 1626 by four more printers: Labayen in Pamplona, Cormellas and Liberòs in Barcelona, and Bidelli in Milan (see bibliographical descriptions in Appendix II). Fernández-Guerra and Menéndez y Pelayo described the first two of these editions, and copied a notice of the third from Nicolás Antonio;

Astrana Marín describes all four, but apparently has seen only the first.[27]

Several bibliographical features of these editions deserve attention. The Pamplona edition (abbrev. P) is the only one in which the division of the text into folios follows closely that of editions X and Y from beginning to end. This indicates that P was copied from X or Y. The Barcelona edition by Cormellas (abbrev. C) follows this same foliation in its preliminaries, but no more, which would indicate that at least these pages were copied from X, Y or P. Both P and C reproduce in their preliminaries a letter found in the Zaragoza editions, entitled "El librero al lector" and signed by Roberto Duport, the book-dealer who financed the Zaragoza editions. This means that either one or both must have copied this letter from X, Y or Z, the only other editions which contain it. All four editions published outside of Zaragoza reproduce all of the Zaragoza *aprobaciones* and *licencias*; C adds nothing to these, P adds a few dated in Pamplona, and the Barcelona edition by Liberòs (abbrev. L) and the Milan edition (abbrev. M) share a new *aprobación y licencia* dated Barcelona, June 30, 1626. This document was probably written for L, and later copied into M.

In conclusion, the bibliographical evidence indicates that P was copied directly from X or Y, that C was probably copied from X, Y or P, and that L is the probable source of M.

2. Textual Criticism

As mentioned above in section B, the text of edition Y lacks two passages found in X, and contains seven others not found in X. Edition Z follows the text of Y, but lacks four more passages. Editions P, C, L and M also follow the text of Y, which

---

[27] References as above, n. 10. The Pamplona edition is also described in Antonio Pérez Goyena, *Ensayo de bibliografía navarra* ([Burgos], 1947), I, p. 221, no. 396 (the source used silently is Fernández-Guerra). The Milan edition is described briefly in Eduart Toda y Güell, *Bibliografía espanyola d'Italia* (Castell de Sant Miquel d'Escornalbou [Barcelona], 1929), III, p. 392, no. 4095, but no one has ever seen the copy which Toda y Güell states is in the Biblioteca Nacional de Madrid.

indicates that they were probably copied, directly or indirectly, from Y.

In analyzing the manifest errors in P, C, L and M, I have collated the same sections of the text as was done for edition Z (see n. 26). In these sections of the text, editions P, C, L and M share forty-two manifest errors, which errors are also shared with other editions as follows: with X, Y, Z — 8; with X, Y — 10; with Y, Z — 20; with Y — 4. It will be noticed that, if P, C, L and M were derived directly from X, it would be difficult to explain the twenty-four errors they share with Y to the exclusion of X. If these four editions were derived from Z, the fourteen errors shared with X and Y to the exclusion of Z would require explanation, to say nothing of the 112 unique errors in Z. The implication that Y is the source of the four editions is supported by the fact that all forty-two errors found in the four are also found in Y. As mentioned above, the division of the text of P into folios follows that of Y closely, and this, together with the distribution of manifest errors and of long passages omitted or inserted, can only mean that P was made directly from Y.

Three of the four editions under discussion, C, L and M, share fourteen errors, as follows: with Y — 6; with Y, Z — 5; with X, Y — 3. Since P appears in none of these groups and Y in all, Y must be the source of C, L and M. As mentioned above, the identity of part of the foliation of C and Y, and the presence of Duport's letter in C, indicate that C is closer to Y than is L or M. This relationship is confirmed by the following five errors which Y and C share to the exclusion of L: Y, C — 1; Y, C, Z — 1; Y, C, P, Z, M — 1; X, Y, C — 1; X, Y, C, P — 1.[28]

---

[28] In as wide an area as X, Y, Z and P, C, L, M, there are naturally a few odd combinations and coincidences, as follows: Y, C, P, Z, M — 1 (L corrected a mistake and M made it again); X, Y, P, L—1 (the same process doubled: C corrects, L errs, M corrects again). These two errors are insufficient to disturb the relationships established above by bibliographical evidence and by much more numerous and clearly defined groups of errors. For examples of numerous coincidental errors which do not disturb the filiation of a group of texts, see my book, *The Text Tradition of the* Memorial *"Católica, sacra, real Magestad"* (Lawrence, Kansas, 1958), pp. 25-35, notes.

Editions L and M share an *aprobación y licencia* probably written for L, and they also share nineteen manifest errors, to which M adds forty-two more errors of its own (L contains only two unique errors). Thus M was undoubtedly copied from L.

In conclusion, it seems clear that Y is the immediate source of both P and C, that C is the source of L, and L the source of M.

D. CONCLUSION AND CHRONOLOGY

In analyzing the bibliographical characteristics of all copies of what has heretofore been considered a single edition of the *Política de Dios* (Zaragoza, 1626), it has become apparent that in 1626 three different editions of the *Política* were published in Zaragoza. Two of these editions, although presenting clearly different texts printed from different forms, contain identical titlepages and foliation, and nearly identical division of the text into signatures and folios.

Close examination of the texts of the three Zaragoza editions reveals that the one which I have referred to as X (copies in the Biblioteca Nacional de Lisboa, Biblioteca da Ajuda, and Biblioteca Universitaria de Sevilla) is the first edition, heretofore unknown. The second edition, referred to as Y (copies in the University of Illinois Library, Biblioteca Nacional de Madrid, Biblioteca Universitaria de Zaragoza, and other libraries), was made directly from X, but introduces numerous corruptions into the text. It is this edition which has generally been considered as the first, and which is superficially so similar to the first.

In 1626 three different editions were made directly from the second Zaragoza edition. One of these has been referred to as Z (copies in the Harvard Law Library and the Boston Public Library), and is a very corrupt text published in Zaragoza by the printer of the first two editions. Another edition, P, was printed in Pamplona, and the third appeared in Barcelona, published by Sebastián Cormellas (edition C).

The text of C later became the source of an edition published in Barcelona by Esteban Liberòs, and Liberòs' text was in turn the source of an edition published in Milan by Giovanni Battista

Bidelli. Thus the early version of the *Política de Dios,* with the text in twenty chapters, was published seven different times in 1626. A stemma representing the filiation of these and other editions will be found following Chapter III.

With the filiation of these seven editions established, it is possible to determine in part their chronology. The preliminaries of X contain an *aprobación* dated January 26, 1626, and two *licencias* dated February 11 and 23, 1626, which means that X did not appear until after the last of these dates. Editions Y and C add no new dates, but L, made from C, contains an *aprobación y licencia* dated June 30, 1626. Thus X, Y, C and L appeared one after another between February and July 1626, and M, copied from L, can be assigned to the second half of the year.

Edition Z contains no more dates than X and Y, and since it is not the source of any known edition with further dates, it is not possible to say more than that Z was published after Y, or some time between the late spring and winter of 1626.

Edition P, made from Y, adds the following dates to those of Y: *aprobación*—July 26, 1626; *fe de erratas*—Oct. 2, 1626; *licencia*—Oct. 6, 1626. Thus P probably appeared in October, 1626.

III

QUEVEDO'S AUTHORIZED REVISION
OF 1626

A. TWO SEPARATE EDITIONS

IN THE SUMMER and fall of 1626 Quevedo repudiated the early version of the *Política,* rewrote the entire text, and published an authorized edition in Madrid. Fernández-Guerra described this edition, and his notes have been reprinted by both Menéndez y Pelayo and Astrana Marín (the latter refers the reader to a copy in the Biblioteca Nacional de Madrid).[1] There is another copy in the Escorial, and two more are in the possession of the present writer (one of these last is the copy Fernández-Guerra used, and contains his pencil-marks in the margins). The typographical and textual characteristics of these four copies indicate that they are all examples of a single edition (abbrev. Q).

Edition Q is not the only edition dated Madrid, 1626: there exists in the Biblioteca Nacional de Lisboa a single copy of another edition with the same date (abbrev. R). Although R has the same contents and foliation as Q, there are ten typographical differences on the title page alone, and many variants in the text. Numerous other differences appear in the division of the text into lines, the errors in foliation, the positioning of catchwords and signature marks, and the spacing of the letters in the lines of the text. The errors in foliation are distributed as follows in Q: f. 62 (numbered as 64), and f. 64 (as 62). R re-

---

[1] Aureliano Fernández-Guerra, ed. Quevedo, *Obras* (Madrid, 1852), p. xcii, cols. b-c (*BAE* XXIII); Marcelino Menéndez y Pelayo, ed. Quevedo, *Obras completas* (Seville, 1897), I, 409-410 (Bibliófilos Andaluces); Luis Astrana Marín, ed. Quevedo, *Obras completas: obras en verso* (Madrid, 1943), p. 1374b.

peats these two errors, and adds five more: f. 12 (numbered as 21), 53 (as 52), f. 82 (as 87), f. 87 (as 78), and f. 92 (as 93). It is clear that Q and R are separate editions; moreover, the errors in foliation suggest that R may be a relatively corrupt text copied from Q.

An analysis of the texts of Q and R confirms the filiation suggested by the errors in foliation. While both share fifteen errors, and Q contains a few more unique errors of a type easily corrected, R adds a considerable number of its own errors, and is in general a more corrupt text than Q.[2]

B. THE SOURCE OF THE AUTHORIZED TEXT

The bibliographical characteristics of edition Q are completely different from those of the other 1626 editions, and so offer no indication as to which edition, if any, Quevedo may have used in making his revisions. But the text of Q contains the seven long passages which first appeared in edition Y, and it also lacks the two passages first omitted by Y (see Chap. II, B). This means that Q was probably not made from any text which antedated Y.

Edition Q shares several manifest errors with other editions, as

---

[2] Among the 15 errors which Q and R share are the following (corrections in brackets): "Cosa es en que hasta oy [no] se auía reparado" (Q, R, f. [9v]; Astrana, *Prosa,* Letter from Vander Hammen, p. 1684a); "sea aprorismo [aphorismo]" (f. 3v; *Prosa* i, p. 380a); "crece Christo, y en entrando en él [entrando él] al vmbral" (f. 4r; *Prosa* i, p. 380b—Astrana's text contains this error); "et domus impleta est ex ordere [odore]" (f. 19r; *Prosa* v, p. 388a); "Los vnos sustentan [sustenta] el enemigo" (f. 23v; *Prosa* vi, p. 390a); "en aquéllos es la humildad cautelosa, y es fuerça sea [y esfuérçase a] dissimular" (f. 52v; *Prosa* xiii, p. 404a); "tuuo por precio de su descompostura, fue la cabeça [descompostura la cabeça] del Precursor" (f. 71r; *Prosa* xvii, p. 413b). The following are examples of the unique errors in R, which do not appear in Q: "Nuestro segun [segundo] Teodosio" (R, f. [13v]; *Prosa,* letter from Vander Hammen, p. 1686, col. a); "inuida [inuidia]" (R, f. 1r; *Prosa* i, p. 379a); "milicia [malicia]" (f. 2v; *Prosa* i, p. 379b); "los lugars [lugares] referidos" (f. 6v; *Prosa* ii, p. 381b); "dará materiales con fauor y ocasión del dueño [sueño]" (f. 9r; *Prosa* ii, p. 383a); "otra le [ley] facinorosa" (f. 11r; *Prosa* ii, p. 384a); "la exposición teólaga [teóloga]" (f. 15v; *Prosa* iii, p. 386a); "dicis [dicit] mater eius" (f. 30r; *Prosa* viii, p. 393a); "muchos [mucho] nos permite" (f. 80r; *Prosa* xix, p. 418a); "yo os preporaré [prepararé]" (f. 91r; *Prosa* xxiii, p. 423a); "dixo SESVS [IESVS]" (f. 91r; *Prosa* xxiii, p. 423a).

follows: Q, X, Y, Z, P, C, L, M — 1 error; Q, X, Y, P, C, L, M — 2 errors; Q, Y, Z, P, C, L, M — 3 errors; Q, Y, P, C, L, M — 1 error. Since Q shares a total of seven errors with the combination Y, P, C, L, M, but only three errors with X and four with Z, it would appear that Q was more closely related to Y, P, C, L and M, or to one of these editions, than to X or Z.

While the punctuation of Q is in general very good, it is not faultless, and several errors in punctuation are shared with Y, P, C, L, and M, but not with X. Examples follow (in square brackets I insert the correct punctuation of X):

> Seréis castigados por rebeldes: adelantarse ha el castigo a vuestro fin, y despierta y preuenida en vuestra presunción. La [presumpción la] indignación de Dios fabricará en vuestro castigo escarmiento a los por venir (X, f. 2r; Q, f. [15v]; Astrana, *Prosa,* preliminaries, p. 376b).
>
> Iesús conociendo en sí mismo la virtud que auía salido de sí, buelto a la multitud dixo: "¿Quién tocó a mi, y a mis vestidos?" y negándolo todos. [todos,] Pedro, y los que con él estauan dixeron: "Maestro, . . ." (X, f. 17r; Q, f. 16v; *Prosa* iv, p. 386b).
>
> En estas puertas, que el cerrarlas es cudicia, y el abrirlas interés, la llaue es el presente, y la dadiua [dadiua:] dize Satanás, oponiendo su gouierno al de Christo: "Derramad y hallaréis; comprad y abriros han" (X, f. 79r; Q, f. 95v; *Prosa* xxiv, p. 425a).

It is clear that in the first example, 'despierta' and 'preuenida' modify 'indignación,' not 'castigo,' and in the second example, the clause "y negándolo todos" is a part of the second rather than the first sentence. The text of the third example makes little sense unless the original punctuation is restored.

There are five more examples similar to these three, and in all eight X contains the original correct reading, while Q, Y, P, C, L and M share erroneous punctuation.[3] Eight more passages contain errors which, although not quite so obvious, are nevertheless distributed in the same way among the editions. And

---

[3] The five remaining examples appear in Q, f. 14r, line 16 (*Prosa* iii, p. 385b, line 17); Q, f. 20r, line 12 (*Prosa* v, p. 388b, line 4); Q, f. 56r, line 22 (*Prosa* xiii, p. 406a, line 29); Q, f. 79v, line 21 (*Prosa* xix, p. 418a, line 3); Q, f. 84v, line 12 (*Prosa* xxi, p. 420a, line 38). Edition P corrects two of these errors.

finally, there are thirty-one passages in which the punctuation of X clarifies a passage quite obscure, but not clearly erroneous, in Q, Y, P, C, L and M.

We know that these errors in punctuation, and four of the seven textual errors mentioned above, first appeared in Y, and were then passed on to P, C, L and M; it now appears likely that Q also derived them from Y, either directly or through another edition. Coincidence alone would be quite insufficient to explain the sharing of such large numbers of errors in such a clear pattern of distribution.

In trying to determine which edition was the source of Q, it may be best to proceed by a process of elimination. For reasons of chronology, edition P may be quickly dismissed from consideration, for it did not appear until after October 6, 1626, and the text of Q was read by a censor before August 27, 1626.[4] By the same token, it is unlikely that L, not published until some time after June 30, 1626, was the source of Q (even if Quevedo had worked in haste, it must have taken him some time to complete his extensive revision of the text). And edition M, printed in Milan from L, would certainly not have appeared in time to be of use to Quevedo. Furthermore, although L introduces numerous manifest errors into the text of the *Política,* and M introduces even more, not one of these errors appears in Q. Edition Z contains even more manifest errors than M, and again none of these appears in Q. Z also lacks the four passages mentioned in Chapter II, and it corrects seven of the sixteen errors in punctuation found in Q, Y, P, C, L and M. Had Quevedo worked from Z, these punctuation errors could hardly have reappeared in such numbers, and it is almost certain that some of the missing passages and textual errors introduced by Z would have filtered into Q (Quevedo would have been unable to correct all of them, just as he was unable to correct all of the errors in Y, P, C, L and M).

The two remaining possible sources of Q are C and Y. C is an

---

[4] See chronology in Chap. II, section D, and bibliographical descriptions in Appendix II.

edition which was made directly from Y, and which follows Y so closely that it reproduces nearly all of Y's textual errors or errors in punctuation (even some of the words run together in Y, such as 'furerat,' f. 19v, and 'conuidoricos,' f. 36r, are run together in C). This means that even though Q may have been made from Y, there are no errors shared by Q and Y which do not also appear in C. On the other hand, however close the relationship between C and Y may be, C introduces many new errors in the text and in the punctuation. Had Quevedo worked from C, it is almost certain that some of these errors would have appeared in his authorized text, but none do so appear.

There are nine passages in which the punctuation of C is less clear than that of Y, and in each of these nine, Q follows Y.[5] Q and C coincide in correcting Y's errors in punctuation only four times, and present different corrections three times. In the cases of variation in punctuation without error, Q and C agree and Y varies twice, while Q and Y agree and C varies five times. There are also five textual variants in which Q and Y agree, but C differs. Finally, there is one error in Q which was almost certainly derived from Y rather than from C: "Los maliciosos otro camino siguen que los beneméritos: en aquéllos es la humildad cautelosa, y es fuerça sea dissimular ambición y atreuimiento; y en éstos es santa y encogida" (Q f. 52v; *Prosa* xiii, p. 404a). C here reads correctly "y esfuérçase a dissimular" (f. 34r), while Y shows how the error in Q arose: "y esfuerçasea dissimular" (f. 43v).[6]

[5] The figures mentioned in this paragraph and in the following one are based on an analysis of certain portions of the text, as described in Chap. II, n. 26.

[6] There is one passage in which Q, Z and C appear, at first glance, to share an error: "Diferentes exércitos son los que pagan los príncipes, que los que acompañan. Los vnos traen grandes gastos, los otros grandes victorias. Los vnos sustentan el enemigo, los otros el rey pereçoso y entretenido en el ocio de la vanidad acomodada" (Q, f. 23v; *Prosa* vi, p. 390a). Editions X and Y read 'sustenta,' correct because the subject is 'enemigo' (Quevedo alludes to the practice common in his day of feeding a victorious army from the enemy's supply train, or by requisition in conquered territory). The clause "Los vnos sustenta el enemigo" is independent, and short enough for a typesetter to grasp partially, and to imagine that as in the preceding sentence, the subject of the verb was "Los vnos." Thus

In conclusion, the theory that Y is the immediate source of Q will fit the distribution of textual errors: seven errors are shared by Q with Y, P, C, L and M because Y passed these on to Q, P, C, L and M. (Q corrected forty-two others which appear in Y, P, C, L and M.) Sixteen errors in punctuation, original in edition Y, plus thirty-one additional obscure passages, indicate that Q may have been made from Y. Chronology excludes P, M and possibly L from consideration as the sources of Q; X and Z are excluded because of missing passages, correct punctuation, and in the case of Z, numerous textual errors. In the chapters studied, there are a total of fifty-three differences between Y and C, including errors and variants in the text and the punctuation. In forty-four of these passages Q and Y agree and C differs, and in three passages the three editions differ. There are no instances in which Q and C share to the exclusion of Y a manifest error in the text or punctuation, and the six passages in which Q and C do present the same reading are corrections of errors or simple variation, both of which can easily be explained by coincidence. Thus it is quite certain that when Quevedo made his authorized text, he worked directly from edition Y.

C. INTERPRETATION

It is surprising that the *Política* ran through nine editions in one year, or more than Cervantes' popular *Quijote,* which was printed seven times in 1605. These nine editions are eloquent

---

in terms of filiation, although 'sustentan' is a manifest error, it is also a deceptive reading which by coincidence tempted three separate printers into an emendation which they did not realize was an error. There is a similar case of apparent error in Q and P: Y reads "Y . . . la calumnia, que es de baxo linage, y siempre tus ruynes pensamientos, califica por fiscales los cómplices" (Y, f. 17v; Q, f. 17r; *Prosa* iv, p. 387a—Astrana here offers silently a late emendation). Both Q and P emended 'tus' to 'sus'; this may make the error less startling, but it still leaves the passage meaningless unless the reading of X is restored: "siempre con sus ruynes." Since both editions P and Q were published at the same time, this is another case of coincidental emendation, and not an error which one edition obtained from the other.

testimony of the publishers' response to a popular demand, but what created this demand? Such interest is all the more surprising in view of the fact that present-day critics assure us that the treatise contains no political ideas either new or original in seventeenth-century Spain.[7]

There are reasons connected with Quevedo's career and his other writings which may explain in part the great popularity of the *Política*. Quevedo was a member of the nobility and a knight of the Order of Saint James; during Philip III's reign he had played a sometimes important part in Court affairs as the envoy of the wealthy and powerful Duke of Osuna, then Viceroy of Naples. Although banished from Madrid in 1622, he returned to favor sufficiently to accompany Philip IV on state visits to Andalusia in 1624, and to Aragon and Catalonia in 1626. He was soon to take a large part in the noisy controversy over the patron saint of Spain, suffer banishment, and return to favor once more as the King's Secretary. In short, he was a man whose prominence in literary and political circles would insure a certain public interest in what he wrote.[8]

Although the *Política* was completed in 1621 (see above, Intro., n. 1), it is not known to have circulated in MS form prior to publication in 1626. The more popular *Sueños* and the *Buscón,* however, did circulate widely in MS form during this period: numerous known copies (a great many more MSS have been lost), and several references by other writers to the *Sueños*

[7] On this particular point, see a study by Donald W. Bleznick, "La *Política de Dios* de Quevedo y el pensamiento político en el Siglo de Oro," *NRFH* IX (1955), 385-394; as Mr. Bleznick says, the same point is made in a more general way by Emilio Carilla in *Quevedo: Entre dos centenarios* (Tucumán, 1949), and Osvaldo Lira, *Visión política de Quevedo* (Madrid, 1947). Although highly praised by Astrana in *Verso,* p. 1458, the views of Pedro Pérez Clotet, La *"Política de Dios" de Quevedo* (Madrid, 1928), belong to an earlier generation.

[8] On Quevedo at the Court of Philip III, see my article "Quevedo and the Court of Philip III: Neglected Satirical Letters and New Biographical Data," *PMLA* LXXI (1956), 1117-1126. On Quevedo's activities between 1622 and 1629, see Ernest Mérimée, *Essai sur la vie et les œuvres de Francisco de Quevedo* (Paris, 1886), pp. 73-99.

before they appeared in print testify to the public interest in these satires.[9] And since the *Buscón* ran through three editions in one year and the *Sueños* four, it is clear that rather than satisfying the curiosity of the public, the MS copies only whetted its appetite. The *Política* was the first of these three works to appear in print, and the first major work published by Quevedo (as mentioned above, it appeared shortly after February 23, 1626, while the *Buscón* did not appear until after May 26, 1626, and the *Sueños* not until the following year). In a sense, the *Política* must have enjoyed early in 1626 some of the public interest in Quevedo's works generated by the MS copies of the *Sueños* and the *Buscón*.

The timing of the publication of the *Política* was also fortunate for political reasons (there seems to be no way of knowing whether or not this was intentional). In the first few years of Philip IV's reign, the new government under the Count-duke of Olivares set out to repudiate the policies of Philip III and to persecute his corrupt ministers (it must be admitted that many of them deserved some form of punishment). The dead King's closest associates, such royal favorites and powerful nobles as the Dukes of Lerma, Uceda and Osuna, the Count of Lemos, and Fray Luis de Aliaga, were either on trial for corruption in government, or banished to the provinces, or in prison. Rodrigo Calderón and six other nobles died on the public scaffold, and Quevedo himself was banished to La Torre de Juan Abad, in La Mancha. These prosecutions continued well into the year 1626: the decree banishing Fray Luis de Aliaga to Huete was dated April 22, 1626, and the judicial sentence fining the Duke

[9] My information about the MSS of the *Sueños* is derived from studies which I hope to publish shortly; see a partial and inaccurate list of the MSS in Astrana, *Verso,* pp. 1299-1302. At least three writers made allusions to the *Sueños* before their publication: Francisco Morovelli de Puebla, "Anotaciones a la *Política de Dios,*" in Astrana, *Verso,* p. 973a; Lorenzo Vander Hammen, in his prefatory letter on the *Política,* Astrana, *Prosa,* p. 1686a; Pedro Espinosa, *El perro y la calentura,* in *Obras completas,* ed. F. Rodríguez Marín (Madrid, 1909), p. 186 (a long quotation from the "Sueño de la muerte").

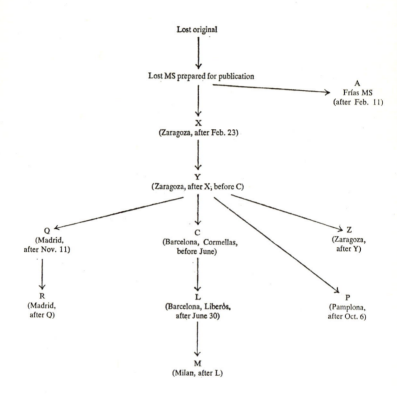

All editions were published in 1626, and the dates
refer to that year

of Lerma one million ducats was handed down in August of the same year.[10] Some of the chapters of the *Política* are devoted to the public punishment of ministers, to the qualities which distinguish good from bad ministers, to the dangers to king, nobles and country of the abandonment of royal power to favorites, to the need for a king to watch his ministers with caution, etc. Philip III had been a very weak-willed ruler who allowed the Duke of Lerma tremendous authority, and whose piety had caused him to be called saintly or angelic; in the *Política* Quevedo asked, "¿Qué importa que el rey sea vn ángel, si los ministros son demonios?"[11] It seems natural that the discussion of such topics in forceful language would find a receptive audience in an atmosphere of public accusation and prosecution of highly-placed men for corrupt practices.

[10] Gregorio Marañón, *El conde-duque de Olivares* (Madrid, 1952), p. 53, n. 6. On Rodrigo Calderón, see Quevedo's penetrating contemporary discussion in "Grandes anales de quince días," Astrana, *Prosa,* pp. 575-581; the best modern study is Angel Ossorio, *Los hombres de toga en el proceso de D. Rodrigo Calderón* (Madrid, [1918]), which contains an extensive bibliography of the MS and printed sources. On Quevedo's banishment, see Mérimée, *Essai,* pp. 73-75.

[11] First edition, f. 61r; in the authorized version, f. 75r, Quevedo substituted "desapiadados" for "demonios"; *Prosa,* chapter xviii, p. 415b.

IV

MANUSCRIPTS DERIVED FROM THE 1626 EDITIONS

A. THE MS SUMMARY OF THE *POLÍTICA*

A MANUSCRIPT exists in the Biblioteca Nacional de Madrid which contains on four folios a short summary of the *Política de Dios* (MS 1092, described below in Appendix II, and edited in full in Appendix I). Each paragraph of this MS consists of a brief summary of the contents of one chapter of the *Política*. The paragraphs are not comprehensive and well-balanced recapitulations, but rather brief notes on some, but not all, of the principal arguments and examples presented in the various chapters. Many phrases are copied verbatim from the *Política,* and these are not always the central point of an argument, but often some particularly striking political admonition, or merely the opening words of a long quotation, or a name or reference which calls to mind a piece of documentation or a line of argument. The paragraph summarizing Chapter II is typical: "Nadie a de estar tan odiado del rey que en su castigo no le haga alguna misericordia. Math. 8, Marc. 5, Luc. 8. Qui autem habebat demonium. Que echándole del cuerpo de vn hombre, rogándole el demonio a Xpo., alcanzó dél que se entrasse aquella legión en los puercos. Fol. 12."

The first sentence of this paragraph is the title of Chapter II, which in the full text of the *Política* reads as follows: "Nadie ha de estar tan en desgracia del rey, en cuyo castigo, si le pide misericordia, no se le conceda algún ruego" (text from the first edition, f. 12v). With the exception of the words "en desgracia," the first clause of the title is copied out verbatim in the MS Summary, while the second clause is condensed. The references to the three gospels are part of the title, and the words "Qui autem habebat demonium" open a long quotation at the very beginning of the chapter. The last sentence in the paragraph is an abbreviated version of the most prominent example used in the chapter to illustrate the principle announced in the title (even the devil received from Christ "alguna misericordia"). There are other points discussed in Chapter II, and there is another long quotation, but these the author of the Summary does not mention.

It seems certain that a MS such as this would not have been made originally by a scribe set to copy out a text, but rather by someone who made notes or extracts as an aid to his memory (perhaps in order to be able to recall the contents of the book at a later date, after the copy used was no longer available).

Information about the author of the Summary may be gathered from a series of Latin quotations in which the text of this MS differs from the *Política de Dios* and the Vulgate. Just as in Spanish, there are of course simple blunders such as 'tentareretur' for 'tentaretur' (chapter xviii), a case of dittography. In the phrase "quod cum vidissent discipulos, increpabant illos" (xii), the nominative 'discipuli,' subject of 'vidissent,' becomes 'discipulos' by the attraction of 'illos.'

Another type of change, however, could only have been made by someone who knew Latin. In the sentence "Erat autem quidam homo ibi triginta et octo annos" (*Política* xiv; John v.5), the word 'annos' clearly expresses duration, but the Summary reads 'annis,' a mistake likely to have been made by someone who knew just enough Latin to confuse the ablative, which expresses the time when something occurred, with the accusative of duration. Again, in the sentence "Afferebant autem ad illum et infantes, ut eos tangeret, quod cum viderent discipuli, increpabant illos" (*Política* xii; Luke xviii.15), the Summary reads 'vidissent,' a change in meaning so slight as to be easily confusing to someone who knew Latin ('vidissent,' pluperfect subjunctive, means 'when they had seen,' while 'viderent,' imperfect subjunctive, means 'when they saw'). When the author of the

Summary copied out what appears in the full text of the *Política de Dios* as "Sequebantur: seguíanle," he wrote "Sequebantur ei" (xvi), and when copying other quotations he sometimes abbreviated quite properly by omitting the verb 'sum': "Tunc Jesus ductus [est] in desertum" (xviii), and "Quidquid calcas rossa [est]" (epilogue by Vander Hammen).

In addition to knowing some Latin, the author was apparently quite familiar with the New Testament. In Chapter V of the *Política,* Quevedo quotes as follows from John xviii.10: "Simon ergo Petrus habens gladium eduxit eum, et percussit pontificis seruum, et abscidit auriculam eius dexteram." Although Quevedo does not mention the name of the servant, nor quote the next sentence from St. John ("Erat autem nomen servo Malchus"), the author of the Summary inserted the servant's name, presumably from memory: "Pedro fue tan baliente a la vista de su Señor que quitó la vida a Malco." (The error in saying that St. Peter took Malchus' life is striking, but not more careless than several others in this MS.) In Chapter XII, the author inserted a reference to "Matthew xviii," and the fact that it should read "xix" might indicate that it was made from memory. In Chapter VIII, the quotation "Vade Satana" (Math. xvi.23, Mark viii.33), addressed by Christ to St. Peter and quoted by Quevedo in the *Política,* is followed in the Summary by the words "et non habebis partem mecum," also addressed to St. Peter, but in a completely different context and in a different gospel (John xiii.8). In Chapter XI, the quotation "ait Petrus ad Iesum" (*Política,* and Luke ix.33), becomes "Petrus dixit ad Jesum" (Math. xvii.4).

All of these variants indicate that the author knew the four gospels well enough to quote them from memory, but not quite well enough to avoid small mistakes in references, and the confusion of different passages which contained some superficial similarity. Further evidence of an interest in the New Testament may be seen in the regularity with which there appear in this short MS all of Quevedo's principal references to the gospels. It seems that a person as familiar with Latin and with the New

Testament as was the author of the Summary would in all probability have been an ecclesiastic.

It is interesting to note that in MS 1092, the Summary of the *Política* is located among documents dealing with ecclesiastics. It is preceded by copies of a group of letters by Cristóbal Collantes, S. J., on the death of Martín de Acuña, Father Confessor of Pedro Téllez Girón (first Duke of Osuna, d. 1590), and followed by a copy of a letter from Philip IV to Pope Urban VIII, and another by Fray Hernando del Castillo, Prior of Our Lady of Atocha (Madrid), both dealing with matters of ecclesiastical administration. Although I am not an expert in paleography, both the Summary and the letter of Philip IV seem to me to be written in the same hand.

Before the significance of the Summary can be evaluated, it is necessary to determine in so far as is possible the source of the text. It is clear that the source was a text similar to the early version of the *Política* (Zaragoza, 1626), rather than to the authorized revision (Madrid, 1626): the title contains the words "tiranía de Satanás," and the text is divided into twenty numbered chapters rather than twenty-four, and contains several significant passages which appear in the Zaragoza version, but are wholly lacking in the authorized revision.[1]

For all but the last of the chapters summarized, there is a folio reference, and these references obviously reflect the foliation of the source of the text. There is no known MS or edition which contains precisely this foliation, but ten of the nineteen

---

[1] The passages are as follows: "al que por todo el reyno reciue y por ninguno halla [read "habla"], al que llama pródigo al rey porque da a otros, y justificado y santo por lo que a él le dexa tomar, al que haze méritos para sí y incombenientes que paren las mercedes de los otros, al que cerca los oydos del rey de hombres y consexeros comprados, que alabándole a él y acrecentándole su gouierno halagan con lisonjas benenosas la perdición y afrenta de los beneméritos" (chapter xiii); "es vn príncipe desfauorezido y que puede poco con su hechura" (xiii); and the citation "Josu. 1. 7" (letter from Vander Hammen). In addition, there is one manifest error which appears in the summary and the Zaragoza version, but is corrected in the revised edition: 'Juuides' for 'Juuiles' (letter from Vander Hammen).

references, including the first two and the last two, correspond exactly to the foliation of the first and second editions (Zaragoza, 1626) and the two editions published in Pamplona (1626 and 1631). The nine references which differ are scattered throughout all of the chapters; in four of them the author of the Summary raised the folio number by one, perhaps because these four chapters begin on the verso of a folio, and with the book open at that place, one might write down by mistake the number which appeared on the facing page. Of the remaining five references, one is an obvious error because it reduces the contents of Chapter IX from eight folios to one, and the others involve changes of one or two folios.[2]

In considering whether the Summary was made from one of the four editions mentioned above, it should be said that one cannot expect the standard of accuracy of the folio references to be higher than that of the rest of the text, which in the case of this MS is quite low: there are five misnumbered chapters, three others not numbered at all, two errors in foliation, and nineteen manifest errors in the text itself, most of which are rather simple blunders: 'cuerpos' for 'puercos' (chapter ii), 'vida' for 'vista' (v), 'pemitir' for 'permitir' (vii), 'los ministro' for 'los ministros' (xii), etc. Thus it is probable that those folio references which do not agree with the Zaragoza and Pamplona editions are mistakes made by the author or a scribe in copying one of the four editions.

There is some evidence that the date of the copy of the Summary found in MS 1092 should be placed after 1629, for on the same page as the end of the text (folio 185r), there appears the copy mentioned above of a letter written by Philip IV to

---

[2] There follows chapter by chapter a list of the folio references in the summary, and in parentheses, the foliation of the first and second editions printed in Zaragoza (both 1626) and in Pamplona (1626 and 1631), all four of which editions share identical foliation: f. 5(5r), 12(12v), 17(16v), 19(19r), 22(22v), 24(24v), 30(29r), 33(31v), 34(39r), 43(42v), 47(47r), 50(50r), 54(53r), 60(60r), 63(62v), 65(66r), 69(68v), 71(71r), 75(75r). As mentioned above, the summary contains no folio reference for Chap. XX.

Pope Urban VIII on September 2, 1629. The handwriting of this letter appears to me to be very similar to that of the Summary (the ink, however, may have been different). Thus it seems most probable that this copy of the Summary, but not necessarily the original, was written after 1629.

In conclusion, this MS consists of a series of notes or extracts of each chapter of the *Política,* probably made by an ecclesiastic who used as a source either the first or second Zaragoza edition (1626), or one of the Pamplona editions (1626 and 1631). While this copy of the Summary appears to have been made after 1629, it is not certain that it was not copied from an original MS of earlier date.

B. THE ROUEN MS

In the Bibliothèque de la Ville de Rouen there exists a complete MS in 225 folios of the First Part of the *Política de Dios* (MS Leber 894 [3049]). This MS came to Rouen from the rich library of Jean Michel Constant Leber, an early nineteenth-century bibliophile.

The source of the text is not hard to find, for the titlepage contains a statement which could only have been copied from the titlepage of the edition of the *Política* published in Barcelona in 1626 by Esteban Liberòs: "Con lizencia en Barcelona. Por Esteuan libreros [*sic*] en la calle de S. Domingo. A costa de Lluch Durã, Y Iacinto Argemir, Libreros." The preliminaries contain an *aprobación y licencia* written for the Liberòs edition, and many of the errors which first appeared in that edition are found in the MS.[3] (These errors were also passed on from the

---

[3] The following are examples of the errors shared by the Liberòs edition and the Rouen MS (corrections in square brackets): "La [Le] aclamaron rey" (MS f. 36v; ed. f. 6v; *Prosa* ii, p. 381b); "nemo [ne me] torqueas" (MS f. 51r; ed. f. 11v; *Prosa* iii, p. 384b); "Ius summum summam [summa] sepae [saepe] malita [malitia] est" (MS f. 53r; ed. f. 12v; *Prosa* iii, p. 385a; the error 'sepae' also appears in earlier editions); "hasta [basta] a hazer" (MS f. 62v; ed. f. 15v; *Prosa* iv, p. 387a); "quia fuerat [fur erat]" (MS f. 67r; ed. f. 17r; *Prosa* v, p. 388a); "coasejero [MS 'coasajero,' for 'consejero'] de hazienda" (MS f. 70r; ed. f. 18r; *Prosa* v, p. 388b); "quasi qui victima [victimat] filium" (MS f. 221r; ed. f. 70r; *Prosa* xxiv, p. 426a).

Liberòs edition to the Milan edition, but the Rouen MS cannot have been copied from the Milan edition because it shares no unique characteristics with that edition, but several with Liberòs.)

The MS is on the whole a faithful copy of its source: although the scribe reproduced many of the more difficult errors in Liberòs' text, he corrected others, and introduced very few new errors and variants.[4] The punctuation, however, is less reliable than the text itself, for clauses or phrases are sometimes interrupted by colons, and sentences terminated with commas.

Perhaps the most striking feature of the Rouen MS is its appearance. It was obviously copied with great care in a beautiful and artistic italic hand, with decorated capitals, much ornamentation, and no cancellations.[5]

[4] The following are examples of errors in Liberòs' text which the scribe of the Rouen MS corrected (corrections in square brackets): "No admirió [admitió]" (MS f. 47r; ed. f. 10r; *Prosa* ii, p. 383b). "lo supo hazez [hazer]" (MS f. 50r; ed. f. 11r; *Prosa* ii, p. 384a); "en los yestidos [vestidos]" (MS f. 63v; ed. f. 16r; *Prosa* iv, p. 387a); "reclicar [reclinar] la caueza" (MS f. 69r; ed. f. 17v; *Prosa* v, p. 388b). Some of the errors introduced in the MS are as follows: "Era [Erat] autem Parasceue Paschae" (MS f. 33r; ed. f. 5r; *Prosa* ii, p. 381a—this passage is missing in the authorized version); "en su coraçón prendiesse [pretendiesse] mayoría" (MS f. 47r; ed. f. 10r; *Prosa* ii, p. 383b); "que los [lo] dexasse entrar" (MS f. 52r; ed. f. 12r; *Prosa* iii, p. 384b); "era mudar solamente [era mudar lugar solamente]" (MS f. 56r; ed. f. 13v; *Prosa* iii, p. 385b); "en los limpios [impíos]" (MS f. 57r; ed. f. 13v; *Prosa* iii, p. 386a).

[5] The lengths to which the scribe went to avoid cancellations may be seen in the following passage, in which he copied the phrase "diole sabiduría de todos los partos de los elementos," as "diole sabiduría de todas las cossas, digo de todos los partos, de los elementos" (MS f. 41v; *Prosa* ii, p. 382b).

V

FROM 1627 TO 1655

I N 1655 there appeared in Madrid an edition of the *Política de Dios* which contained for the first time the unpublished Second Part of the treatise. This complete text of both parts, published ten years after Quevedo's death by a printer who had access to his manuscripts, became the sole source of all succeeding editions until the middle of the nineteenth century, when Fernández-Guerra reverted in part to the 1626 texts. Thus although the *Política* was published many times in the seventeenth and eighteenth centuries, the 1655 edition is the last which may offer new source material for the text.

The history of the text between 1627 and 1655 begins with a statement made in 1700 by the printer and bibliographer, Pascual Bueno, to the effect that the Second Part of the *Política* was published in Madrid in 1627.[1] Fernández-Guerra has correctly rejected this notion (*BAE* XXIII, p. xciii, col. a), but it is of course impossible to say that Pascual Bueno was not mistakenly referring to some edition of the First Part which has since been lost. It may also be that the date 1627 is an error for 1628, the date of a lost edition published in Madrid.

Although no copy has survived, evidence suggesting that the *Política* was published in Madrid in 1628 may be deduced from the preliminary material of a hitherto unknown edition published at Salamanca in 1629 (hereinafter referred to as edition S; copies are listed in Appendix II). Edition S contains two *aprobaciones* dated respectively September 4 and 26, 1627, a *privilegio* dated November 28, 1627, and a *tasa* dated January 24, 1628. These dates follow a normal sequence: a *privilegio* was not granted until the *aprobaciones* had been obtained, and

[1] Pascual Bueno, ed. Quevedo, *Providencia de Dios* (Zaragoza, 1700), f. [8r], "El impresor al que leyere."

the *tasa* was the last item to be drawn up, save the *fe de erratas*.[2] All of these preliminary items were signed in Madrid, not Salamanca, but all are completely different from those found in Quevedo's authorized edition (Madrid, 1626). Furthermore, the *tasa* states that the book contained fourteen signatures, a number not found in any known seventeenth-century edition, including S. Since S contains no official preliminaries other than those listed above, it may be safe to assume that its text was taken from an edition published in Madrid in 1628, and that it reflects the principal features of such an edition.

The Madrid edition would thus have contained the early Zaragoza version of the *Política,* with the text in twenty chapters. It is also possible to say that since S contains certain passages which appeared for the first time in the second Zaragoza edition and its descendants, the Madrid edition of 1628 was not copied from the first Zaragoza edition.[3] Finally, since S shares none of the unique errors found in any of the known descendants of the second Zaragoza edition, the Madrid edition of 1628, as the source of S, was probably made directly from this second Zaragoza edition.

Although there is nothing in edition S to identify the printer of the Madrid edition, it should be said that in 1632 the playwright Juan Pérez de Montalbán mentioned in his *Para todos* that an edition of the *Política* had been published in Madrid by Pedro Tazo.[4] Since Montalbán's citation will not fit any early edition known today, he may have been referring to the Madrid edition of 1628.

[2] Agustín González de Amezúa y Mayo, "Cómo se hacía un libro en nuestro Siglo de Oro," in his *Opúsculos histórico-literarios* (Madrid, 1951), I, 333, 341, 354, 358.

[3] The passages characteristic of the second Zaragoza edition are discussed in sect. B of Chap. II.

[4] Juan Pérez de Montalbán, *Para todos* (Pamplona, 1702), p. 518, "Indice de los ingenios de Madrid" (first edition in Madrid, 1632). In assigning a date to the edition mentioned by Montalbán, Fernández-Guerra inexplicably suggests 1633, one year after Montalbán's notice (*BAE* XXIII, p. xcv, col. c), while Astrana Marín prefers 1627, presumably because Pascual Bueno mentioned that date (*Verso,* p. 1376a).

Aside from the information it provides about other editions, the Salamanca text is interesting because it was evidently a simplified or popular version, purged of all Latin and of most long or difficult words, and with many passages completely rewritten. Most of this revision of the text is such clumsy and often erroneous work that it is highly improbable that Quevedo had any hand in it. There is no way to discover whether or not these characteristics of the Salamanca edition reflect the form of the Madrid edition of 1628.

In 1629, the year that the Salamanca edition appeared, Pedro de Lacavallería published in Barcelona an edition of the *Política* in which he took pains to punctuate the text carefully, and to correct a very large number of its errors. The result was an unusually pure text printed in very clear type, all the more surprising in view of the fact that, as will be seen below, it was made from one of the relatively corrupt early editions. The preliminaries of Lacavallería's edition are identical with those published by Esteban Liberòs in an earlier edition (Barcelona, 1626): the special *aprobación y licencia* written for Liberòs appears, and the article entitled "El librero al lector" is missing, as it is in the Liberòs edition.[5] Although the division of Lacavallería's text into folios does not follow closely that of any known edition, there is one error which may be significant: 'Aprosopolepsia,' a Greek word written in roman letters, appears as 'Aprosolopsia' (f. 11v), an error apparently derived in part from Liberòs, who misspelled it as 'Aprosopolopsia' (f. 12r). There are in addition several variants shared by these same two editions to the exclusion of all others.[6]

In 1630 the Portuguese printer Mathias Rodrigues published in

---

[5] These features are also present in an edition made from Liberòs' text and published in Milan in 1626, but although the Milan text is very corrupt, it does not share any of its numerous errors with the Lacavallería edition, and so was almost certainly not the source of the latter.

[6] Examples follow (the readings of the other editions appear in square brackets): "saber de su [saber su] secreto" (Liberòs f. 10r; Lacavallería f. 9v); "quien te [me] tocó" (Liberòs f. 16r; Lacavallería f. 14v); "lo dé a [los] pobres" (Liberòs f. 40r; Lacavallería f. 36v).

Lisbon a unique conflate edition of the *Política,* taking part of his text from the early Zaragoza version and part from the authorized version (Madrid, 1626). From the authorized version Rodrigues took his titlepage, and the three new chapters of that version (he printed these one immediately after another, and not spaced between the chapters of the early version, as had Quevedo). Since half of the errors found in these three chapters are also found in the second edition (1626) of the authorized version, but not in the first, it is clear that the second authorized edition was the ultimate source of the Lisbon text of the three chapters. The fact that Rodrigues took only the titlepage and the three new chapters from the authorized version, without renumbering the first chapter, adding any of the preliminaries, or spacing the three chapters according to that version, may suggest that his immediate source for the items in question was not a complete printed copy of the authorized edition, but merely a manuscript transcription of the titlepage and the three chapters.

For the remainder of the text, and all of the preliminaries, Rodrigues followed the Zaragoza version, including the position of the chapter entitled "En el gobierno superior de Dios sigue al entendimiento la voluntad." (Although in the Zaragoza version this chapter was a part of the preliminaries, Quevedo made it the first chapter in the authorized version.) With respect to filiation, the Lisbon edition lacks three of the four passages omitted in the third Zaragoza edition (see Chap. II, sec. B and n. 25; the fourth passage occurs in a quotation from the *New Testament* which the printer could easily have restored). Since in addition much of the division of the Lisbon text into signatures and folios follows that of the third Zaragoza edition, and there is a series of errors shared exclusively by the two editions,[7] it seems clear that the third Zaragoza edition was

[7] The following are examples of these errors (text as in the Zaragoza edition, with my corrections in square brackets): "le escribieron [inscribieron] rey" (edition Z and Lisbon ed., f. 1v; *Prosa* ii, p. 381a); "Math. 32 [22]" (Z, Lisbon, f. 3r; *Prosa* ii, p. 381a—omitted in this version); "infirmi esse meus [essemus]" (Z, Lisbon, f. 10v; *Prosa* iii, p. 385b, n.1); "Meterse [metióse] en lo que no le tocara" (Z, Lisbon, f. 16r; *Prosa*

the source of such parts of the Lisbon text as were not derived from the authorized version.

A number of Quevedo's works were printed in Pamplona in 1631, among them the *Política de Dios*. This edition was quite certainly made from the Pamplona edition of 1626: it contains all of the preliminaries and many of the variants and errors found only in that edition.[8] Moreover, the division of the text into signatures, and often into folios, is the same (this is not true, however, of the preliminaries).

Although Luis Astrana Marín mentions an edition of the *Política* which appeared in Madrid in 1641 (*Verso,* p. 1387b), he does not identify the source of his information, and I have found no other reference to the edition. The presence of the words "tiranía de Satanás" in the title would indicate that the text probably followed the early Zaragoza version, but it is difficult to say more about the edition and its probable source because Astrana describes neither text nor foliation.

Fernández-Guerra mentions an edition entitled *Política de Dios y Govierno de Christo,* published in Warsaw in 1647.[9] This title, if correctly transcribed, would indicate that the text followed the authorized version, and so would probably have been made from one of the two editions published in Madrid in 1626. Although Fernández-Guerra had not seen a copy of the Warsaw edition, nor has anyone since his time, there is some circumstantial evidence to the effect that such an edition did exist. The publisher, and the place and date of publication, are described by Fernández-Guerra as follows: "Varsoviae, In Officina Petri Elert S. R. M. Typographi, Anno Domini, 1647." It is

---

v, p. 388b); "Respondiéndole [Respondiéndoles] Iesús, les dixo" (Z, Lisbon, f. 39r; *Prosa* xiii, p. 404a); "Rey que oy cree [oyere] esta petición" (Z, Lisbon, f. 43r; *Prosa* xiii, p. 406b, n.1).

[8] The following are examples of errors and variants peculiar to the Pamplona editions (corrections in square brackets): "aquí se [le] llama" (f. 21r); "ducientos [docientos] ducados" (f. 25r); "no prouar [aprouar] el govierno" (f. 47r).

[9] *BAE* XXIII, p. xcvii, col. c, no. 68 (Fernández-Guerra adds with neither explanation nor qualification, "una reimpresión más de la príncipe"). *Verso,* p. 1389a, n.97.

known that Peter Elert was an active printer in Warsaw at this time, that he was in fact the crown printer, and that he often signed his titlepages with the exact words quoted by Fernández-Guerra, varying the year of course. Furthermore, between 1640 and 1660 Elert was one of the very, very few Polish printers who published any books in Spanish and Italian, in addition to Latin and Polish. Since the titlepages of the books which he printed in Polish were signed in that language, the Latin signature recorded by Fernández-Guerra probably means that the edition was printed in Latin or Spanish.[10]

In 1648 the bookdealer Pedro Coello and the printer Diego Díaz de la Carrera, both of whom had printed several books for Quevedo before his death in 1645, began the publication of a series of collections of his works. Among the volumes published in Madrid, often with much duplication of material and little planning, were a collection of prose and some verse entitled *Enseñanza entretenida y donairosa moralidad* (1648), the *Parnaso español* (1648), the *Primera parte de las obras en prosa* (1649), *Todas las obras en prosa* (1650, published with Tomás Alfay), and the *Política de Dios,* complete in two parts (1655). In the last two years of his life Quevedo had complained that Coello and Díaz de la Carrera were careless;[11] in spite of the access they undoubtedly had to Quevedo's manuscripts through

---

[10] Numerous books published by Peter Elert are listed in Karol Estreicher, *Bibliografia Polska* (Krakow, 1882), VIII, 237-284 (Chronological List, 1455-1799; Alphabetical List in Vols. XII-XXIX). Among such books are a *Dictionarium Hexaglosson, cum multis colloquijs* [French, German, Italian, Latin, Polish, Spanish], (Varsoviae, in offic. Petri Elert, S. R. M. typ. Anno D. 1646); Carlos Bonyeres [*sic*], Baron de Auchy, *Epitome floreado de los comentarios de Caio Julio Cesar* (Varsoviae, in Officina Petri Elert, S. R. M. typographi. Anno Domini 1647); Carlo Bartholomeo Piazza, *La fama reale ovvero il principe trionfante Vladislao Quarto . . . , Monarca della Polonia* (in Varsovia, per Pietro Elert, Stampatore Regio, 1647); Albert Borghesi, *Il santo Stanislao consecrato a monsig. illustrissimo, reverendissimo Giorgio Tiskiewicz, vescovo di Samogitia* (in Varsovia per Pietro Elert, Stampatore di Sua Maestà [1648]). These are the only books in Spanish and Italian which Estreicher lists as published in Poland between 1640 and 1660.

[11] The complaints appear in a series of letters written in 1644 and 1645, which may be seen in *Prosa*, pp. 1865-1875, "Epistolario."

Joseph González de Salas and others, their negligence and in-attention are unfortunately all too apparent in the works pub-lished posthumously.

The text of the *Política de Dios* appears in the *Enseñanza entretenida,* but without a proper title: in the index it is listed as "Govierno superior de Dios, i tiranía de Satanás," a conflate reference composed of part of the title of the first chapter of the authorized Madrid version, followed by part of the title of the early Zaragoza version; in the text, the treatise appears under the heading "Capítulo primero," followed by the title of the first chapter.

It is clear that the text of the 1648 edition follows the author-ized version: there are twenty-four chapters, and all of the extensive textual alterations characteristic of that version appear in the 1648 edition. Since none of the numerous errors intro-duced by the second edition of the authorized version appears in the 1648 text, this text must have been made from the first edition of that version (Madrid, 1626).

Not all copies of the 1648 edition display the same textual and typographical characteristics. While the discussion of the three sets of preliminaries and the complicated differences be-tween individual copies may be left for the bibliographical de-scriptions in Appendix II, it should be said here that there are two different editions, one represented by copies in the Biblio-teca Nacional de Madrid, Biblioteca Central de Barcelona, and the author's collection (hereinafter referred to collectively as edition B), and the other by a single copy in the Kongelige Bibliotek, Copenhagen (hereinafter referred to as edition K). On almost every page of these two editions there are variations in punctuation, accentuation, spelling, the use of abbreviations, the positioning of letters, and the division of the text into lines. These differences are sufficiently numerous to prove conclusively that the editions were printed from different settings of type.[12]

---

[12] Although Fernández-Guerra at first attributed to a single copy the preliminaries of one edition and the foliation of another (*BAE* XXIII, p. xcviii, col. a, no. 71), he later stated that there existed two editions

But since the order of the contents in both is identical, as is the division of the text into signatures, pages, columns, and often lines, it is clear that one of the two was made directly from the other.

The filiation of the two editions can be established in several ways. In the first place, although the page references in the table of contents are the same in both editions, the pagination of the text is not. The difference occurs on pages 236 and 330, each of which pages falls between two articles, and was left blank in edition B; in K there are no corresponding blank pages. This means that between pages 236 and 329 the pagination of K is lower by one number than that of B, and from page 330 to the end of the volume, the pagination is lower by two numbers. Since the page references are the same in both tables of contents, it is obvious that the compositor of K copied the table of contents of B, but then in setting up the corpus of the text, he not only failed to leave pages 236 and 330 blank and so threw the pagination off, but also failed to correct the references in the table of contents (in all probability, it had already been printed).

The suggestion that edition K may be the second of the two editions is supported by the citations in the *Fe de erratas*. The same eleven errors are listed in both editions, but while in B three of the eleven are actually correct in the text itself, in K nine are correct. Since the errors involved are all simple and easily corrected blunders, the distribution of corrections would seem to indicate that the *Fe de erratas* was composed originally for the edition with three corrections, and later copied word for word into the second edition, with no regard for six more errors which the compositor of the second edition had corrected while setting up the text.

(*Política de Dios,* ed. Fernández-Guerra, Madrid, 1867, I, xviii, n. 1). Menéndez Pelayo, using Fernández-Guerra's notes, describes only one edition, but with a non-existent foliation (Quevedo, *Obras completas,* ed. Menéndez Pelayo, Seville, Bibliófilos Andaluces, 1897, Vol. I, pp. 440-441, no. 85), and Astrana Marín has copied Menéndez Pelayo's notes (*Verso,* p. 1389b, no. 99).

Further evidence of the filiation is furnished by a comparison of the manifest errors in the two 1648 texts of the *Política de Dios* with those in their source, the first authorized edition (Madrid, 1626). Of twenty-four errors analyzed in the 1626 edition, twelve reappear in edition B, but only nine in K.[13] We know that one of the two 1648 editions must have been made from the other; if K were the first, and corrected all but nine of the errors in the text of its source, it would be difficult to explain how B, copied directly from K, reinstated three of the early errors not found in K. If on the other hand B were the first edition, it would not be surprising that K could improve slightly on the number of errors corrected by B.

Thus the page references in the table of contents, the citations in the *Fe de erratas,* and the errors in the text of the *Política* suggest that edition B was the source of K.

Although no bibliographer has ever seen a copy of the *Primera parte de las obras en prosa* published by Pedro Coello in 1649, it is known that the *Política de Dios* was not among the works contained in this volume.[14] The next year, however, the *Política* was published by Tomás Alfay and Diego Díaz de la Carrera in *Todas las obras en prosa* (1650).[15] As in the *Enseñanza entretenida,* the text of the 1650 edition follows the authorized version in twenty-four chapters, including all of the extensive al-

[13] The three errors of the 1626 text which appear in B but not in K are as follows (I follow the text of B, with K in square brackets): "Crece Christo, y cn entrando en el al vmbral [entrando en el vmbral] remitido de los pontífices, dizen los euangelistas" (B, p. 261a; K, p. 260a; *Prosa* i, p. 380b); "Domus impleta est ex ordere [odore] vnguenti" (B, p. 272b; K, p. 271b; *Prosa* v, p. 388a); "Para echar aquellos cudiciosos mohatreros, dizen [dize] san Iuan que hizo vno como açote" (B, p. 315a; K, p. 314a; *Prosa* xix, p. 417a).

[14] Fernández-Guerra lists the contents of the *Primera parte* in *BAE* XXIII, p. xcviii, col. b, no. 74, but states that he had not seen a copy. Astrana Marín copies Fernández-Guerra's notes in *Verso,* p. 1390b, no. 104, and Amédée Mas states that he has not seen a copy (ed. Quevedo, *Las zahurdas de Plutón,* Poitiers, 1956, p. 28b, "Étude bibliographique").

[15] The second volume of this edition, as unknown to recent bibliographers as the first, is entitled *Prosiguen todas las obras en prosa,* and was published in 1650 by Pedro Coello and the widow of Juan Sánchez, and bound with the first volume. Copies are listed in Appendix II.

terations introduced by that version. And again as in the *En-señanza,* the text of the *Política* was published with neither title nor preliminaries (in the table of contents of this volume, how-ever, the title does appear correctly). Since the 1650 edition contains none of the numerous errors and variants introduced by the second authorized edition in 1626, or by either edition of the *Enseñanza* in 1648, the text was evidently taken directly from the first authorized edition. This conclusion is supported by the following error, which is shared exclusively by the first authorized edition and the 1650 edition (my correction is in square brackets): "Potestis bibtre [bibere] calicem quem ego bibiturus sum?" (1626 ed., f. 57r; 1650, p. 144; *Prosa* xiv, p. 406b). The fact that this error is of a type relatively easy to correct, makes its presence in the two editions all the more strik-ing and significant.

As mentioned above, the 1655 edition of the *Política* con-tained both the First Part and the unpublished Second Part, and became the source for almost all succeeding editions until the middle of the nineteenth century. In this edition the text of the First Part follows the authorized version in twenty-four chapters, with all of the extensive alterations introduced by that version. But contrary to what had been done in 1648 and 1650, the printer this time took pains to include the correct title of the treatise, and all of the pertinent preliminary material, including several summaries of the 1626 *aprobaciones.* (He was not, how-ever, as careful as he might have been, for some of the pre-liminaries of the First Part were assigned to the Second Part.) Naturally, the texts of these extensive preliminaries could only have been obtained from the 1626 editions, and in fact the 1655 text shares no errors or variants with the second authorized edition (1626), nor with the editions published in 1648 and 1650. The theory that the text of the First Part of the 1655 edition was made directly from the first authorized edition is confirmed by one error which these two editions share, but which is corrected in all others: "Legio nihi [1655: 'nihil'; others: 'mihi'] nomen est" (1626 ed., f. 12v; 1655, p. 13; *Prosa* iii, p.

384b; 'nihil' is obviously a clumsy attempt to correct 'nihi').

In concluding the present review of the editions of the First Part of the *Política de Dios* published between 1627 and 1655, it is interesting to note the decline in popularity of the treatise. Nine editions were published in 1626, and for the next five years new editions continued to appear at the rate of approximately one each year. After 1631, however, interest in the *Política* declined markedly, and only one edition was published in Spain between that date and the appearance of the first edition of Quevedo's collected works in 1648. During these years Quevedo was producing other works which absorbed the interest of the public, such as *La cuna y la sepultura* (seven editions in 1634) and the *Carta al serenísimo Luis XIII* (six editions in 1635),[16] to say nothing of the *Sueños,* the *Buscón* and the *Vida de Marco Bruto.* After 1648, the *Política* began to appear in print again in the numerous collections of Quevedo's works published during the next two decades. In this period there was also a certain interest in the treatise itself, as witnessed by the editions published in 1655, 1662, and 1666 (two).

It is surprising that the publication in 1626 of Quevedo's own revised text in a good edition had no discernible effect on other editions for twenty-two years: all of the editions published in Spain between 1627 and 1648 followed the early version which Quevedo had rejected. In the case of those published in Barcelona and Pamplona (1629 and 1631), the printer possibly found it easiest to take his text from an edition which had been printed by himself, or in his own city. But it is not so easy to understand why an edition published in Madrid in 1628, with official *aprobaciones* and *licencias,* and a full *privilegio* issued to Quevedo, should not follow the text for which Quevedo had been granted a different ten-year *privilegio* in 1626.[17] Perhaps

[16] Most of these editions are listed in Astrana, *Verso,* pp. 1382-1384, and the rest are mentioned by Quevedo himself in a letter to Sancho de Sandoval, *Verso,* p. 1505.

[17] The *privilegio* of the 1626 authorized edition is printed only in summary form in that editon, but the summary states that it was issued to Quevedo for ten years, for a book entitled *Política de Dios, gouierno de*

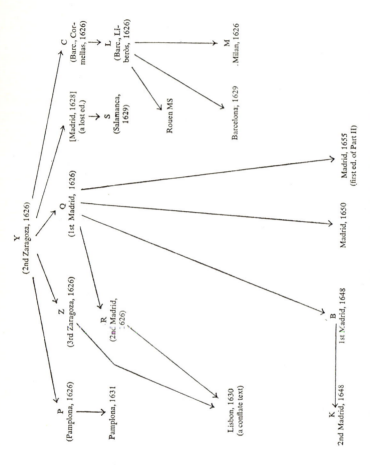

Texts not shown are either of indefinite filiation (Madrid ed. of 1641, and the MS Summary), or appear in the stemma at the end of Chapter III (first ed. and Frías MS).

the fact that the Portuguese printer Mathias Rodrigues wished
to include the material added in the authorized edition, but apparently could locate no printed copy of this edition, is an indication that such copies were more difficult to find than copies of
the early version.

Although Quevedo lived for nineteen years after the publication of the authorized edition of the *Política,* there is no evidence that he ever made further revisions or alterations in the
text. The source of the text of every edition of which a copy
is known today can be identified, and none of the texts contains any alterations which would indicate Quevedo's intervention. This is of course not surprising, in view of his known indif-
ference at this time to the fortunes of his own works.[18]

When Pedro Coello and Diego Díaz de la Carrera compiled
their editions of the *Política* in 1648, 1650 and 1655, they undoubtedly had access to Quevedo's manuscripts, but they either
found no new material for the First Part of the *Política,* or
decided not to use any they did find. At any rate, the texts of
their three editions were taken directly from the authorized
edition of 1626.

Christo, and signed by Sebastián de Contreras in Madrid on October 1,
1626. The *privilegio* of the 1628 edition, printed in full in the preliminaries of that edition and of the Salamanca edition of 1629, was issued
to Quevedo for twenty years, for a book entitled *Política de Dios,
gouierno de Christo, y tiranía de Satanás,* and was signed in Madrid by
Pedro de Contreras on November 28, 1626.

[18] Quevedo's friend Lorenzo Vander Hammen commented on this in-
difference in a letter dedicating Quevedo's *Desvelos soñolientos* (Zaragoza, 1627), to Francisco Jiménez de Urrea (*Desvelos,* f. [4r]; *Prosa*
p. 1697a).

VI

THE MANUSCRIPT AND PRINTED VERSIONS OF THE SECOND PART OF THE *POLÍTICA DE DIOS*

THE TEXT TRADITION of the Second Part of the *Política de Dios* is very different from that of the First Part. Only two sources are known, a MS now in the Royal Academy of History in Madrid, and an edition. These two texts differ so widely that one can only presume the loss of several intervening MSS, one or more of which effected changes far more fundamental and extensive than those found in the 1626 revision of the First Part.

Little precise information exists about the chronology of the Second Part. The Academy MS is an undated seventeenth-century copy, not an autograph, but in its final chapter there is a reference to the sack of the Flemish town of Tirlemont by the French Huguenots under Marshal Châtillon.[1] Since this incident occurred in June, 1635, and is referred to in the MS as occuring "en estos días," it seems clear that the final chapter of the version represented by the MS was written very soon after the events mentioned—perhaps in the summer of 1635.[2]

---

[1] MS, chap. viii, sec. 1, f. 366v; 1655 edition, chap. xxiii, sec. 1, p. 327; Astrana Marín, *Prosa,* xxiii, sec. 1, p. 518b. On the sack of Tirlemont by Marshal Châtillon (Gaspard III de Coligny, 1584-1646, named Marshal of France in 1622, but known as Marshal Châtillon), see H. Pirenne, *Histoire de Belgique* (Brussels, 1911), IV, 276. On the vigorous Spanish reaction to this attack, see Quevedo's *Carta a Luis XIII,* and José María Jover, *1635: Historia de una polémica y semblanza de una generación* (Madrid, 1949).

[2] In chap. iii of the MS (f. 333r; ed. xvii, p. 250; *Prosa* xvii, p. 485b), there is a reference to a "Jubileo Grande" declared by Pope Urban VIII. Fernández-Guerra, in a note reprinted in *Prosa,* p. 485b, states without citing his source that "se publicó en Madrid a 18 de Mayo de 1634,"

The edition of the Second Part was first published in Madrid in 1655, ten years after Quevedo's death. It was apparently ready for publication in 1652, for on June 20 of that year the text was approved by one of the official censors, whose certificate appears in the preliminaries. With respect to the date of composition of this version, there appears in Chapter XX the following reference to Philippe d'Arenberg, Duke of Arschot, who while on a diplomatic mission to the Spanish Court was imprisoned in Madrid: "Dios guarde a Vuestra Magestad, que en esto ha dado exemplo a todos los reyes de su tiempo quando en materia tan ardua y temerosa se cerró con el duque de Ariscot, gran señor en Flandes, y le oyó, y vio, y acercó a sí con piedad magnánima, de que espero resultará a él libertad con perdón, y a Vuestra Magestad gloria con seguridad."[3]

Since Arschot was arrested in Madrid on April 16, 1634, and died in prison on September 24, 1640,[4] the fact that Quevedo ex-

---

which, if true, would fix the date of composition of almost all of the Academy MS. But the Jubilee Years are declared only every 25th year, and I have found no record of an extraordinary Jubilee in 1634 or 1635 (not even in the detailed *Cartas de algunos padres de la Compañía de Jesús,* in the *Memorial histórico español,* ed. Real Academia de la Historia, Madrid, 1861, Vol. XIII). Quevedo was surely referring to the Jubilee which Urban VIII declared in 1625 (see Jolanda de Blasi, *Il giubileo: Racconto di sei secoli e mezzo,* Florence, 1950, p. 350; Miss Blasi mentions no other Jubilee between 1625 and 1650). Fernández-Guerra, who relied heavily on Antonio León Pinelo's "Historia de Madrid," may have been referring mistakenly to the plenary indulgence granted by Urban VIII on Sept. 17, 1634, to all who visited Our Lady of Atocha in Madrid on certain occasions (León Pinelo, Biblioteca Nacional de Madrid, MS 7748, f. 299v; see also the *Cartas de Jesuitas,* XIII, 98, letter of Sept. 19, 1634). I cannot explain the date of May 18, 1634, in Fernández-Guerra's note (there are no references in the *Cartas de Jesuitas* to any special religious celebrations in May of 1634). I owe my information about the MS of León Pinelo's "Historia" to the kindness of Don José Antonio Martínez Bara, Conservador de la Sección de Consejos, of the Archivo Histórico Nacional in Madrid.

[3] 1655 ed. xx, p. 281; *Prosa* xx, p. 499a.

[4] The date of Arschot's arrest is given as "a medio de mayo" in three MS copies of Antonio de León Pinelo's "Anales o Historia de Madrid:" Biblioteca Nacional de Madrid, MS 1764, f. 299r; MS 7748, f. 289; MS

presses hope for his prompt release must mean that this passage was written between 1634 and 1640.

Two more events of a historical nature may further define the period of composition. First, the *terminus a quo* can probably be advanced to late in 1635, if not 1636, because as we know Quevedo was writing the final chapter of the MS version of the Second Part in the summer of 1635, and presumably he finished this before beginning to work on the expanded version (on this filiation, see below). And secondly, the *terminus ad quem*, at least for the material preceding the reference to the Duke of Arschot in Chapter XX, was probably December 7, 1639, the date on which Quevedo was arrested summarily in Madrid, and all his papers confiscated. Most of the papers were returned upon his release from prison in 1643, including the MS of another treatise, the *Primera parte de la vida de Marco Bruto,* which he had written before 1631. In the prefatory material to the edition of the *Marco Bruto* which Quevedo published in 1644, he listed all the papers which had not been returned in 1643,[5] but did not mention

---

2925 (not 2295), f. 225r (my friend Don José Antonio Martínez Bara has generously supplied me with this information). Fernández-Guerra in a note reprinted by Astrana Marín in *Prosa* xx, p. 499a, accepts León Pinelo's date. But it is known that León Pinelo often used secondary sources, and wrote the "Anales" piecemeal long after the the events related (the chapters on the years 1572-1621, for instance, were written between 1640 and 1648—see Ricardo Martorell's edition of these years of the "Anales," Madrid, 1931, p. 14). On the other hand, the date of Arschot's arrest is confirmed as April 16, 1634, in two independent contemporary documents, both of which furnish abundant details about the conversations between Arschot and the King on the day the former was arrested: *Cartas de Jesuitas,* in the *Memorial histórico español,* XIII, 38-41, and Matías de Novoa, *Historia de Felipe IV,* in *Colección de documentos inéditos para la historia de España* (Madrid, 1878), LXIX, 358-366. Further confirmation in H. Pirenne, *Histoire de Belgique,* IV, 266. The date of Arschot's death, Sept. 24, 1640, appears in Josef Pellicer de Ossau y Tovar, *Avisos históricos,* in the *Semanario erudito,* ed. Antonio Valladares de Sotomayor (Madrid, 1790), XXXI, 218. In the *Cartas de Jesuitas* there is a reference made on Sept. 29, 1640, to Arschot's recent death (*Memorial histórico español,* XVI, 6).

[5] *Prosa,* pp. 691b-692a.

any MS of the expanded version of the Second Part of the *Política de Dios*. This may well mean that such a MS of the expanded version was returned to him in 1643.

The Academy MS of the Second Part of the *Política* is nearly as long as the First Part, and is divided into eight chapters. To these eight, the expanded version found in the edition of the Second Part adds fifteen more short chapters, bringing the total length of the printed text to just over twice that of the MS. This difference in length, however, does not mean that the MS is a fragment: on the contrary, it is a complete copy of a certain state or version of the Second Part, with a full title, a lengthy dedication, a long note to the reader, and the full text for each chapter presented. In addition, the MS ends with a short and original statement in which the author expresses his loyalty to the King and the Church, and explains why "I finished this work" ("acabé esta obra").[6]

The general outlines of the order of priority of these two texts have been established above by historical criteria. The immediate problem is to carry forward this analysis by textual criteria, and to establish in so far as is possible the relationship between the two texts. (No direct relationship can be discovered because the two are so widely separated by such basic characteristics that neither one can have been copied directly from the other.)

The eight chapters of the MS are numbered in order, and there is a certain continuity in the material presented. The first chapter deals with the origin of the institution of monarchy, the second with the birth of a king, and the third with the qualities necessary in a child king. Chapter IV deals with the relationship between a king and his favorite, Chapters V and VI with other ministers and subjects, and the two final chapters respectively with royal councils and military affairs.

[6] MS viii, sec. 2, f. 395v; 1655 ed. xxiii, sec. 2, p. 362; *Prosa* xxiii, sec. 2, p. 533b.

A different type of continuity may be observed in the sequence of the persons whom Quevedo addresses in the text. Although the Second Part of the *Política* was dedicated to the Pope, in the text Quevedo addresses the King of Spain as well as the Pope, perhaps because the treatise was clearly written as advice for the King (the early version of the First Part had been dedicated to the Count-duke of Olivares, but addressed to Philip IV; the 1626 revision was similarly addressed, but dedicated jointly to Philip IV and Olivares). In the Second Part, the Pope and the King are not usually addressed simultaneously: in the first five chapters of the MS Quevedo addresses the Pope, in the sixth "Señor" (a title he used for either the Pope or the King), and in the last two chapters "Vuestra Majestad."[7] In his final statement at the end of the MS, Quevedo does not mention the Pope at all, but says that he wrote the Second Part to honor God and the Church, and to serve the King.

I do not believe that this change in the person addressed need cause surprise, especially if, as seems possible, the Second Part was composed over an extended period of time. Quevedo himself, in dedicating the MS version to Pope Urban VIII, discussed the universal authority of the Church, and wrote as follows: "La ley de Dios a de juzgar a las leyes: no las leyes a Dios. Yo, Beatísimo Padre, que empecé el primero a discurrir para los reyes y príncipes por la vida de Christo, llena de magestad en todas sus acciones, lo prosigo en entrambas espadas."[8] I believe that "el primero" in the sense of "at first" refers to the First Part of the *Política,* "lo prosigo" to the Second Part, and "entrambas espadas" to ecclesiastical and civil power.

The eight chapters of the MS are not found in their original sequence in the edition, nor even in a single group. They are scattered in disorder throughout the fifteen new chapters, with

---

[7] This pattern is broken only in Chap. II, when in the midst of many passages addressed to the Pope, Quevedo addresses the King twice (MS ii, f. 332r; ed. xvi, pp. 247, 248; *Prosa* xvi, p. 484, cols. a, b).

[8] MS, Dedication, f. 320r; ed. f. [15r]; *Prosa,* p. 430a.

the exception that the first and last chapters of the MS appear
as the first and last of the edition:

	MS	Edition
Chapter	I	I
	II	XVI
	III	XVII
	IV	XIX
	V	XVIII
	VI	IX
	VII	XV
	VIII	XXIII

This distribution interrupts the continuity of the subject matter
observed in the MS, without substituting any readily discernible
order in the new form of the text. Furthermore, the chapters
added in the edition are all addressed to "Vuestra Majestad,"
which means that the pattern of change from Pope to King noted
in the MS is lost. When the first chapter of the MS version was
prepared for printing, all six references to the Pope were omitted,
but in the preparation of the other chapters of this version,
such references were not omitted, with the result that some
groups of chapters are addressed to the Pope, and others to the
King.[9] The disruptive effects of the changes in the order of the
chapters and the sequence of the persons addressed in the text
suggest that the MS may be an early version which was later
broken up and inserted piecemeal into a longer text.

Further evidence in favor of the priority of the MS may be
found in many of the variants which appear in the printed text
of the eight original chapters. References in the MS to Pope
Urban VIII (d. July 29, 1644) have been changed in the edition

[9] The changes in the persons addressed in the MS have been described
above. In the edition, Chap. i (also i in the MS) is addressed to "Señor,"
Chaps. ii-viii to "Vuestra Majestad," Chap. ix (vi in the MS) to "Señor,"
x-xiv to "Vuestra Majestad," xv (vii in the MS) to "Vuestra Majestad,"
xvi-xix (ii, iii, v, and iv respectively in the MS) to "Santísimo Padre," xx-xxii
to "Vuestra Majestad," and xxiii (viii in the MS) to "Vuestra Majestad."

to Alexander VII, and such changes can only have been made
after Alexander's election to the Papacy on April 7, 1655, ten
years after Quevedo's death. These changes include the insertion of an entirely new final page in the Dedication, and a long
paragraph at the beginning of Chapter III (XVII of the edition),
both of which passages contain much adulation of Pope Alexander. It is tempting to think that two other passages which appear only in the edition but do not mention Alexander by name
may be similar insertions, for they are equally adulatory in
tone, and their presence interrupts the flow of the discussion.[10]

While it is certain that Quevedo did not write the references
to Pope Alexander VII, and possible that he did not write the
two similar passages just mentioned above, it is difficult if not
impossible to decide the question of attribution in the case of
many other variant passages. It is not axiomatic that every
alteration which seems to us to be an improvement must therefore be attributed to the author, nor is it axiomatic that every
corruption must be attributed to someone other than the author.
Quevedo himself, for example, may have wished for reasons
not now known to us to alter or destroy the continuity of the subject matter of the MS version (as mentioned above in the Introduction, seventeenth-century Spanish political treatises were not
usually systematic in this respect). The point which is at issue
here, and which can be decided separately from the question
of attribution, is the order of priority of the two texts of the
Second Part.

In addition to the four passages referring to the Pope, the
printed text of the first and second chapters contains three other
passages not found in the MS. These take the form of asides,
explanations, or additional information, which may suggest that

---

[10] The final page of the Dedication may be seen only in the 1655 ed.,
f. [15r-15v], and in other early editions (Fernández-Guerra and Astrana
Marín have omitted it because the early editions state that Quevedo did
not write it). The long paragraph at the beginning of Chap. III is on
f. 333r of the MS; ed. xvii, p. 250; *Prosa* xvii, p. 485a-b. The last pair
of passages mentioned above are in Chap. II (ed. XVI), MS f. 327v; ed.
pp. 237, 238; *Prosa* xvi, p. 480 a-b.

they were late accretions to the MS version. Examples follow (I have placed the material in question in square brackets):

> A éstos enuía ángeles, porque velan [¡ O causal! en tus experiencias provechosas se libra la salud del pueblo)] y guardan vigilias de la noche (MS ii, f. 328r; ed. xvi, p. 239; *Prosa* xvi, p. 480b).

> Chrisóstomo [(eloquentísimo abogado, voca de oro en la estimación de la de todos los padres griegos y latinos)], en la *Homilia ad Neophytos,* tratando de los doctores de la Iglesia en comparación de las estrellas y de los santos, dice, "Aquéllas . . ." (MS ii, f. 329r; ed. xvi, p. 241; *Prosa* xvi, p. 481b; there is another example on this same page).

In the first example quoted, the inserted clause clearly interrupts the syntax. In the second, the clause which begins "tratando . . ." is necessary for an understanding of the material about to be quoted, while the inserted clause is not.

In the eight original chapters, there are four cross-references found in both the MS and printed texts, and five more which appear only in the latter. Six of these nine references are of little interest because they refer to the First Part of the *Política,* or are otherwise correct in both versions of the Second Part. One of the remaining references, however, reads as follows (Quevedo is discussing the life of St. John the Baptist): "Cosa admirable, que en toda su vida no hubo otra cosa sino peligros y tentaciones y cárcel y muerte. Vnos le ofrecen el mesiazgo, que era el reyno; otros le preguntan si es él, y lo dexan en su voluntad. El capítulo pasado todo fue peligros, que los fabores y mercedes preferidas para la verdad no son otra cosa" (MS v, f. 342r; ed. xviii, p. 257; *Prosa* xviii, p. 488b).

In the MS, this reference occurs in Chapter V, and the "capítulo pasado" referred to is Chapter IV, which deals extensively with Saint John the Baptist. But as mentioned above, the chapters of the MS were reorganized in the printed version, and Chapter V became Chapter XVIII. Contrary to what might be expected, Chapter IV was placed after V, and so appears as Chapter XIX. This means that the "capítulo pasado" in the printed version refers to a chapter which was numbered III in the MS, and which has nothing to do with Saint John the Baptist. It is thus most probable that this reference was originally written for a version in which the chapters were numbered and arranged as they are in the MS, and that later on, when the chapters were renumbered and rearranged, the reference escaped correction.

The two remaining cross-references appear only in the printed version of the eight original chapters. The first is in the form of a marginal note, and the second is an insertion which I have set off below in square brackets:

> Hácese capítulo particular de este sucesso en el capítulo 13 desta 2 parte, a diferentes ponderaciones (ed. ix, p. 183; *Prosa* ix, p. 457a, with this note omitted).

> Christo Nuestro Señor, sólo y verdadero rey, nació obedeciendo el edicto de César, que mandó registrar todo el orbe: "Exiit edictum a Cesare Augusto vt describeretur vniuerssus oruis." [(Sobre cuyo lugar se hizo ya discurso en otro capítulo, de que se puede llamar parte muy essencial éste al mismo propósito.)] Vino Ioseph de Nazaret, ciudad de Galilea, a Betleen, . . . (ed. xvi, pp. 235-236; *Prosa* xvi, p. 479a; the reference is to Chapter X of the edition).

Since both Chapters X and XIII appear only in the printed version, it is clear that these two references were not inserted into the text until after that version had been written. Moreover, they were evidently inserted by someone who took some pains to explain and justify the repetitious citation of a few Biblical passages, and the consequent duplication of some of the discussion. They are similar in tone to the following marginal note found in Chapter XIII of the edition: "Queda romanzado en el capítulo 9 desta 2 parte, y así no se repite en éste" (ed. xiii, p. 210; *Prosa* xiii, p. 468b, n. 1). If Quevedo himself was aware of the duplication pointed out in these cross-references, it certainly did not trouble him much, for a great number of such passages appear in the Second Part (they were apparently the Biblical passages for which he had a certain predilection). Although it is difficult to determine the attribution of the cross-references (the author himself may have changed his mind about the duplication after completing the Second Part, perhaps because of some criticism unknown to us), it is most unlikely that Quevedo wrote the following unique evaluation found in a marginal note to Chapter XX: "Este capítulo es mui notable en su materia, y digno de ser leído con toda atención" (ed. p. 274; *Prosa* p. 495b, n. 2).

It is thus probable that of the numerous passages which are found only in the printed text of the eight original chapters, at least nine appeared as accretions late in the history of the text. These are the four references to the Pope, three explicative passages, and two cross-references. Further evidence that the edition is the later of the two versions may be found in the cross-reference which is correct in the MS but erroneous in the edition.

There is in addition another series of alterations which may furnish further evidence of the relationship between the two texts of the Second Part. Some of these alterations improve the clarity of the text presented in the edition. They do not involve correction of manifest errors, but rather elucidation of instances of ellipsis, anacoluthon, or *lectio difficilior*. The following example may be cited (I have placed in square brackets the words substituted in the edition): "Fueron referidas las palabras que avía dicho Dauid a Saúl, a cuia presencia siendo lleuado [al qual, siendo llevado a su presencia], dixo [muy] animossamente Dauid . . ."[11]

In the printed text, a few tautological expressions are removed, and the meaning clarified, as follows (as above, square brackets indicate the changes): "Grandes misterios aguardaban años auía este suceso. Desempeñó este suceso [Desempeñó de] muchas profecías . . ." (MS iii, f. 334v; ed. xvii, p. 253; *Prosa* xvii, p. 486b). . . . "Esto creió y tubo la ydolatría ciega en

[11] MS viii, sec. 1, f. 374v; ed. xxiii, sec. 1, p. 336; *Prosa* xxiii, sec. 1, p. 522a-b. Further examples in the same chap. and sec., MS f. 364r; ed. p. 325; *Prosa* p. 517a; and MS f. 366r; ed. pp. 326-327; *Prosa* p. 518a.

más obserbancia que ninguna otra cossa. No trata de otra cossa
[Trata dello] Balerio Máximo . . ." (MS viii, sec. 2, f. 391r; ed.
xxiii, sec. 2, p. 357; *Prosa* xxiii, sec. 2, p. 531a). In describing a
woman who brought a jar to a well to draw water, Quevedo wrote
as follows: "A quien venía a sacar agua, a quien venía [traía] con
qué dar y sacar lo que se le pidiese . . ." (MS vi, f. 352v; ed. ix, p.
184; *Prosa* ix, p. 457b; further examples in this chapter, MS f.
349r and 349v; ed. p. 180; *Prosa* p. 456a).

The edition, in several passages, simply omits strong criticism
found in the MS (contrary to previous practice, I use square
brackets here to indicate the readings of the MS):

> ¿Cómo pues acertarán los reyes, que no lo siendo [que siendo
> suma ignorancia (como lo es todo hombre y más los reyes, que
> tanto son de proueccho a los que los asisten al lado, quanto
> ignoran)], ni oyen ni quieren oír, ni preguntan . . .? (MS iii, f.
> 334v; ed. xvii, p. 254; *Prosa* xvii, p. 487a).

> Desde que los reyes consiente priuanzas, desechan las con-
> juraciones y leuantamientos por necios y arriesgados. [¿Qué falta
> hacen las comunidades, donde ay que se leuante con el rey?] A
> César y a Tiberio . . . (MS v, f. 343; ed. xviii, p. 259; *Prosa*
> xviii, p. 489a-b).[12]

The fact that these alterations were made in the interest of
clarity, precise expression, and moderate criticism, suggests that
they are part of a revision of the text rather than a first draft.

I believe that the complex of different characteristics discussed
above indicates that the text of the MS represents an early version or first draft of the Second Part of the *Política de Dios,* and
the edition a later revision, much enlarged.

This conclusion need not imply that the text of the MS is
purer than that of the edition. Neither contains an appreciably
higher percentage of errors than the other, and the fact that
there are almost no errors shared by both indicates that they are
separated by several lost texts. We simply do not know, for instance, how many handwritten copies intervened between the

[12] Another example in MS iv, f. 339r; ed. xix, p. 269; *Prosa* xix, p. 493b;
and two more in MS v, f. 342r; ed. xviii, p. 258; *Prosa* xviii, p. 489a).

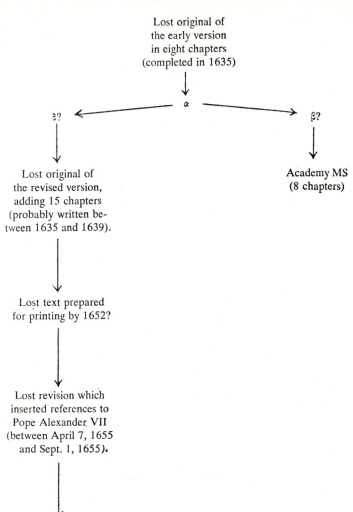

Lost original of
the early version
in eight chapters
(completed in 1635)

α

ε?

β?

Lost original of
the revised version,
adding 15 chapters
(probably written be-
tween 1635 and 1639).

Academy MS
(8 chapters)

Lost text prepared
for printing by 1652?

Lost revision which
inserted references to
Pope Alexander VII
(between April 7, 1655
and Sept. 1, 1655).

First edition
(Madrid, after
Oct. 7, 1655).

Academy MS and the original autograph, nor do we know the history of the text between the early version and the later revision. It may even be that almost all of the printed text was taken from a source much closer to the original than the source of the Academy MS.

I believe that it can be said that the edition is not a lineal descendant of the MS. A comparison of both texts reveals that the MS contains at least four instances of haplography, which probably could not have been restored in any text made directly or indirectly from the MS. The following examples may be cited (I enclose in square brackets the words missing in the MS):

> En esta Junta, Consejo y Conçilio se congregaron pontífices y phariseos, por donde fue de las más graues que ha hauido. . . . Y siendo esto assí, en el votar todos, menos vn pontífice llamado Cayfas, [no saben lo que se dizen, ni lo que se piensan. Y Caifas,] que sólo supo lo que se dixo, no supo lo que se deçía, fue mal presidente y pareçió buen profeta (MS vii, f. 359r-359v; ed. xv, p. 230; *Prosa* xv, p. 477a).

> La lisonja mañosa gana albricias con los poderosos cuando les dice: "Yermo está el rey, desierta la magestad; todos acuden a ti." [Y si bien entienden éstos que valen (sic) la palabra "todos acuden a ti,"] caueza es de proceso: el que se lo dice, más le acusa que le aplaude (MS v, f. 342v; ed. xviii, p. 258; *Prosa* xviii, p. 488b.)[13]

If the edition is not even an indirect copy of the MS, it must be concluded that its source was a text not now known, but derived ultimately, in the eight early chapters, from one of the sources of the MS itself.

---

[13] Further examples as follows: "Los thesoros an de estar abiertos para Dios, y assí los an de traer los reyes. [¿Qué serán los reyes] que a Dios le [MS: "les"] quitan los suyos?" (MS ii, f. 330v; ed. xvi, p. 243; *Prosa* xvi, p. 482b). "Y no contento con esta repetición, 'dicit ei tertio: Simon Ioannis, amas me? [Contristatus est Petrus quia dixit ei tertio, Amas me?'] ¡ Qué perseuerante tenía Pedro la memoria . . ." (MS, Dedication to the Pope, f. 319r; ed. f. [13v]; *Prosa* p. 429a). In the second line of the first passage quoted above, I have emended the text of the MS, which reads "de las más graues que hauido."

APPENDIX I

A CRITICAL EDITION OF THE MANUSCRIPT SUMMARY OF THE *POLÍTICA DE DIOS* (BIBLIOTECA NACIONAL DE MADRID, MS 1092, FOLS. 182R-185R)*

Politica de Dios, gouierno de Xpo, tirania de Satanas.
D. Fran^{co} Queuedo.
Pregon y amenaza de la Sauiduria. Fol. 1.
Pontifices, emperadores, reyes, principes:
5 A v.^{ro} cuidado no a v.^{ro} aluedrio, os encomendo las gentes
Dios (Sapientia 7), y os dio trabajo y afan honrosso,
no vanidad ni descanso.
Cap. 1. Que Xpo. supo ser rey, y nacio en tanta pobreza
y viuio en ella. Fol. 5.
10 Nadie a de estar tan odiado del rey q. en su castigo no le
haga alguna misericordia. Math. 8, Marc. 5, Luc. 8.
Qui autem habebat demonium. Que echandole del   Cap. 2
cuerpo de vn hombre, rogandole el demonio a Xpo.,
alcanzo del que se entrasse aquella legion en los
15   puercos. Fol. 12.
A de dar a entender el rey que sabe lo q. da y tambien lo
q. le tomã. Math. 9, Marc. 5, Luc. 8. La muger q. toco   Cap. 3
la vestidura de Xpo. con fe de q. si la tocasse sanaria
de la sangrelluuia q. tenia, y en tocandole dixo Xpo.,
20   "Quis me tetigit?" Y que entienda q. el que se la toma
no lo ignora. Fol. 17.
Al rey nada se le a de quitar, aunq. sea para socorrer las
necesidades de los pobres. Juan. 12. Maria ergo accepit   Cap. 4
libram vnguenti nardi. ¿Que dixo Judas? El que dize

---

* In this edition, the spelling, accentuation, and division of the text into paragraphs remain as in the original; the punctuation (very poor in the original), capitalization, and the separation of words have been modernized. For all other changes, the reading of the original appears in the footnotes.
6. The letter *S* of 'Sapientia' is written over a small *c*.
9. After the word 'viuio,' the words 'en ella' were written in at the end of the line, crossed out, and written again on the next line.
14. MS: en los cuerpos.

que se quite de la authoridad del rey, se vendiesse por   25
treinta dineros para repartir a los pobres. Judas es el
que dize que se quite de la authoridad del rey para
repartir a los pobres. Y quitallo del labrador, del bene-
merito, del huerfano, de la viuda, en quien se repre-
senta Xpo., para otras cosas, ese vendera al rey como   30
Judas a Xpo. Y buscar arbitrios son mohatras de
sangre humana, q. para hazerse assi quieren empo-
brezer al rey y al reyno. Fol. 19.

    La persona del rey es el effecto de lo q. manda. Juan 18.
Pedro fue t[a]n baliente a la vista de su señor q. quito   35
Cap.   5   la vida a Malco, y en faltandole la vista de Xpo., le
nego por vna pregunta de vna mozuela. Rey q. trauaja
delante de los suyos los obliga.

    Y si no puede estar [el rey] en todas partes personal-
mente, imbie generales que manden con la persona y   40
obras, no con la pluma. Y no basta q. el rey este presente si duerme. Luc. 8. Duerme [Christo] y preuiene
la tormenta: todo se turba. Durmio aunq. sabia la
borrasca, para ver la fe de los suyos. Y quando los suyos le dexan dormir y repossar, y solicitan el silencio,   45
sus mangas estan haziendo, y mucho mas si dispierto
esta dormido en las cossas. Fol. 22.

    Christo no remitio memoriales, y vno que remitio a los
dicipulos lo descaminaron. Math. 14, Juan 6, Marc. 6,
Luc. 9. Et exiens, vidit. Saliendo, Jessus vio vna gran   50
multitud de gente en el desierto y apiadose dellos, que
[Cap. 6]   de ordinario despiden, no socorren. Hizoles poner en
orden y diolos de comer, que los apostoles los des-
pedian. Quando no les toca algo, todos son escussas y

25. The word 'rey' is written over the word 'que.'
31. MS: mohatra
34. Chapter 5 begins with this line.
35. MS: a la vida de su señor
38. I have transferred the folio number which appears after 'los obliga'
to its correct position at the end of chapter 5.
43. An *m* appears underneath the hyphen of 'tor-/menta.'
46. The spelling 'dispierto,' common in the Golden Age, is perhaps due
to the metaphonic action of the following diphthong (comp. 'tiniente,'
'licion,' 'disierto' and other examples cited with extensive bibliography in
Rodolfo Lenz, *El español en Chile,* trans. Amado Alonso and Raimundo
Lida, Buenos Aires, 1940, p. 265, n. 1).
47. I have transferred the folio number which appears after 'las cossas'
to its correct position at the end of chapter 6.
51. A *d* appears underneath the second *t* of 'multitud.'

55   dificultades. Xpo. con solos cinco panes y dos pezes
satisfaze a tantos; aca con quanto los reyes tienen no
pueden hartar a vno. Fol. 24.

No ha de permitir el rey singularidad en ninguno en
publico, diferenciandose de los demas. Juannis 2. Al   [Cap. 7]
60   tercero dia se celebraron las bodas de Cana Galilea.
No ha de tener en publico el principe, ni con criado,
hermano ni madre, amistad que le desauthorize: Quid
tibi et michi, mulier? Que es causa de desacreditarse.
30.

65   Castigar a los ministros malos en publico es dar exemplos
a imitacion de Xpo., y consentirlos dar escandalo a
exemplo de Satanas, que es descredito de la eleccion,
contrario al primer angel, al primer hombre, a Judas,   [Cap. 8]
      a Sant P[edr]o. Luego los castigo, aunque eran eleccion
70   suya. A Sant Pedro: "Vade Satanas, et non habebis
partem mecum." 33.

Doctrina de Xpo. es no descuidarse el rey con sus
ministros. Es comun lenguage de la adulacion y lisonja
dezir con tirania cosa q. les suena bien a los principes,
75   y los halagan quando los dizen q. bien pueden echarse
a dormir, que los criados tienen a su cargo sus
cuydados. Esta es blasfemia, y no consejo. Xpo. con
sus priuados, a quienes en los mas arduos cassos   Cap. 9
lleuaba consigo al Tabor y al huerto, el velaba y ellos
80   dormian. Haziendo lo contrario, rey que duerme
gouierna entre sueños, y quando mejor le sucede,
sueña q. gouierna. De modorras y letargos de principes adormecidos adolescieron, y mejor diciendo pe-
recieron, graues republicas y monarchias, porq. si ellos
85   duermen, los allegados velan con los ojos cerrados. 34.

58. MS: pemitir
61. An *l* appears under the *u* of 'publico.'
63. The Medieval spelling 'michi' seems to have been frequent in the
17th century (further examples in Milton A. Buchanan and Bernard
Franzen-Swedelius, eds. Lope de Vega, *Amar sin saber a quien,* New
York, 1947, p. 174, note to verse 1964).
85. MS: cetrados, with the *t* written over an *r*. The scribe evidently
corrected what he thought was an error, without realizing that Quevedo's
forcefully ironical point was that "velar con los ojos cerrados" is not
"velar" at all, but "dormir." Thus the sentence would read "si ellos [los
reyes] duermen, los allegados duermen también." The texts of the first edition and the complete MSS support this interpretation.
85. Comparison with chapters 8 and 10, and with the complete text
of the *Política,* indicates that the foliation of chapter 9 should be perhaps 39 or 40 rather than 34.

Pretensores: el rey solo deue atender a sus peticiones.
Math. 20, Marc. 10. Tunc accessit ad Jesum mater
filioɼ Zeuedei. Y oyendolo los diez dizipulos, se in-
dignaron. La ceremonia muestra luego las intenciones.
Peticiones de vanidad presto se conozen. Nescitis quid   90
petatis. El pobre de la piscina: "D[omi]ne, si vis,

Cap. 10   potes me mundare." Este despachalo luego, no re-
mitillo a nadie, que quieren mas para si que para
nadie, y todo se lo toman. 43.

Buen ministro. Math. 17, Marc. 9, Luc. 9. Estaban ren-   95
didos al sueño. Petrus autem et qui cum illo erant.

Cap. 11   Petrus dixit ad Jesum, "Bonum est nos hic esse.
Tibi, Moisi, vnum, et Eliae vnum." El mal ministro
dixera, "Para mi vno, otro para mi, y para mi el
tercero, y todo para mi," porq. Satanas a dicho a sus   100
ministros q. todo es para ellos, y el todo lo permite
a vno. El ministro que pide su reposo, quietud y descanso, tengale siempre por sospechoso el rey. Fol. 47.

Como y a quien se an de dar las audiencias de los reyes.
Math. 18. Afferebant autem ad illum et infantes, vt   105
eos tangeret (Luc. 18), quod cum vidissent discipuli
increpabant illos. Traianle muchachos a Xpo. y en-
fadabanse los apostoles, y dixo Xpo., "Dexaldos venir,
que de estos es el reyno de Dios." Los reyes hazen
todo esto al reues, que no se dan sin interpretaciones,   110
siempre con mala acogida de los ministros, que pareze

Cap. 12   q. aun aquel corto tiempo de la audiencia no le
querrian, si no es para ellos. Esto deue dezir el rey:
"Dexaldos venir a mi." Si Xpo. se recata de sus
apostoles porque entre ellos auia vn Judas, ¿q. haria   115
vn rey de la tierra que apenas entre doze Judas se
halla vn apostol? 50.

Buen criado es del rey el q. se precia de serlo y darle
a su señor lo q. le toca. No es criado ni ministro del
rey el q. affecta la grandeza, con q. descubre q. no solo   120
quiere ser igual, pero mayor q. su señor, imbidioso de su

91. The reference to the "pobre de la piscina" belongs in chapter 14
(the reference in chapter 10 is to a leper).
   101. The first edition and the complete MSS read 'promete' for 'permite.'
   106. MS: discipulos
   110. An *l* appears underneath the first *n* of "que no se dan."
   111. MS: los ministro, que

corona, emulo del poder, con la leche del fauor alimen-
tado, con la soberuia y codicia. Sant Juan Baptista,
buen criado: "Non sum dignus soluere calceamenta."
125   El rey q. llama criado al que le violenta y no le aconse-
ja, al que le gouierna y no sirue, al que le toma y no
pide, al que por todo el reyno reciue y por ninguno ha-   Cap. 13
bla, al que llama prodigo al rey porq. da a otros, y justificado y santo por lo q. a el le dexa tomar, al q. haze
130   meritos para si y incombenientes q. paren las mr̄cds
de los otros, al que cerca los oydos del rey de hombres
y consexeros comprados, que alabandole a él y acrecentandole su gouierno, halagan con lisonjas benenosas
la perdicion y afrenta de los benemeritos; a esse
135   demonio y no criado se llame: este tal no es rey sino
esclauo, es vn principe desfauorezido y que puede
poco con su hechura, y para mayor afrenta permite
Dios las insignias reales.
    Dize vn araue que el rey ha de ser como el aguila; que
140   ha de tener alrededor de si cuerpos muertos; no a de
ser cuerpo muerto que tenga en contorno de si aguilas.
Si los consejos proponen y el criado determina, ¿que
sera sino cuerpo muerto? Y contradize a Dios en dar
la authoridad real a quien Dios no quiso darsela. 54.
145   Para quien nacieron los reyes y a quien han de ayudar.
Juan 5. Erat autem quidam homo ibi triginta et octo
annos, ett [cetera]. Vis sanus fieri? El primer aphoris-
mo de la salud espiritual es la voluntad propia. ¿Que
es vna republica sino vna piscina? Y el rey ha de ser el
150   angel que la mueua para sanar. Estos son los pretendien-
tes, benemeritos, agrauiados y oprimidos, pobres y
viudas, y si el no los remedia, dara ocasion a que venga
Dios a desagrauiarlos. Si esto pasaba en la republica   Cap. 14
de Xpo., ¿q. sera en la de vn rey con cargos y mer-

127. MS: por ninguno halla
129. A *d* appears underneath the *m* of 'tomar.'
133. MS: acrecentandole su su gouierno
138. I have transferred the folio number which appears after "insignias
reales" to its correct position at the end of chapter 13.
145. A *q* appears underneath the word 'a.'
147. MS: annis
150. MS: pretencientes
153. The numeral '14' in the margin is written over '15.'

cedes, q. las mas vezes las rebuelue Satanas, [y los]   155
ministros y diablos, que este nombre tienen los ambicio-
ssos, los souerbios y tiranos? Bueno es q. el rey sea
angel, pero a de serlo para los q. fueren hombres;
con los necesitados, y con su mano a de reuoluer estas
aguas. Fol. 60.   160

Con q. gente se a de enojar el rey en demonstracion
y azote. Joan 2, Marc. 11. Et veniens Jesus in Jeru-
salem, et cum introijsset in templum cepit eijcere ven-
dentes et ementes. El rey a de abrir los ojos sobre los
que en su casa se le quieren hazer cueua de ladrones, y 165
a estos tales, azotes, y derriballes las messas y officios,
Cap. 15   y la prophanan y desauthorizan. El a de ser el
executor de la justicia. Y venden palomas y tortolas
estos: son lo q. quitan la sangre a la viuda pobre y
huerfanos, y persiguen a los inocentes. 63.   170

El rey ha de lleuar tras si los ministros, no los ministros
a el. Sequebant[r] ei. No se lee que Xpo. los siguiesse.
Rey adestrado es ciego; enfermedad tiene, no cargo;
bordon es su cetro; aunq. mira, no ve. El que adiestra
a su rey, peligrosso off[ici]o escoge, pues se atreue al   175
cuidado de Dios: a mucho se auentura si no haze lo q.
Cap. 16   deue. Hauiendolo el rey menester, este tal no le guia,
sino le arrastra; codicia tiene, y no caridad; no
seruicio, sino offensa le haze. Si el rey a de errar,
menos escandalosso es q. yerre por si q. no por otro,   180
q. es desprecio en los subditos. 65.

Quienes son ladrones y quienes ministros. Juan 10.
Ammen, ammen, dico vobis, qui non intrant per hos-
tium in ouili ouium, ille fur est et latro. El que agatea
por la lisonja y trepa por la mentira, y se empina sobre   185

155. In the complete MSS, this line reads as follows: "q. las mas veçes
las rebuelue Satanas, y las mas veces la rebuelben los hombres, y son
mynistros los diablos, que por otro nombre se llaman los ambiciosos . . ."
(Frías MS, 167).

156. Two illegible letters appear underneath the letters *bl* of 'diablos.'

167. Misnumbered as 'Cap 16.'

177. Misnumbered as 'Cap. 17.'

184. Although not listed in Corominas, *Diccionario crítico etimológico,*
the word 'agatar' appears in three early 17th-century dictionaries with
the meaning "to creep on all fours" (Samuel Gili y Gaya, *Tesoro
lexicográfico,* Madrid, 1947). According to Martín Alonso, *Enciclopedia
del idioma,* 'agatar' is used in Salamanca to mean 'trepar por un árbol o
una pared."

la maña y se encarama sobre los cohechos, y biene   Cap. 17
dando y que le roben, a robar viene. No es el mayor
ladron el q. hurta porque no tiene, sino el q. teniendo,
da mucho por hurtar mas; q. el merito, el virtuosso,
190   el q. tiene meritos, por la puerta de su rey entra, y esse
pastor es. 69.

   Al rey que se retira de todos el mal ministro le tienta,
no le consulta. Math. 4. Tunc Jesus ductus in desertum
ab spiritu, vt tentaretur a diabolo. A los solos no ay
195   mal pensamiento q. no se les atreua. Q. haga de
piedras pan, primera peticion; la segunda, q. se arroje   Cap. 18
del pinaculo; la tercera, q. le adore. No es mucho q.
negociando solo se atreua a tanto; no es mucho q. se
hagan adorar los q. a solas negocian. 71.
200   Consejeros, allegados, confesores y priuados de los reyes.
Juan 14. Ego sum via, veritas et vita. Los q. han de
aconsejar a los reyes an de tener estas tres partes: an
de ser guia, verdad y vida. Lo contrario es ser des-   Cap. 19
peñaderos, sendas de lauerintos, ceguedad y confusion.
205   En estos tales esta librada la perdicion de los reyes. 3.°
Regum, cap. 22. Josaphat, rey de Juda. Consejeros q.
con pareceres agenos solicitan el apoyo de sus men-
tiras. 75.

   La differencia del gouierno de Xpo. al gouierno de los
210   hombres. Querite et imbenietis, pulsate et aperiet[r]
bobis. En el reyno del mundo el cerrar las puertas es
codicia y el abrirlas interes, la llaue es el presente y la
dadiba. Esto es de Satanas: derramad y hallareis,   Cap. 20
comprad y abriros han, opuesto a Xpo., porq. vnos
215   engaitan, otros adulan, otros engañan, otros mienten.
Dad y daros han, dad mas y os daran mas. Hurtar
para dar pareze presente y es mercanzia, modo q.
permite Dios para perdicion de ladrones.

*   *   *

  186. Misnumbered as 'Cap. 18.'
  193. MS: no le consuela.
  194. MS: tentare / retur
  196. Misnumbered as 'Cap.19.'
  201. MS: han de ser aconsejar
  203. MS: es ser despinadores. In the margin, 'Cap. 19' is written over
'Cap. 20.'
  213. Misnumbered as 'Cap. 21.'
  216. MS: Dad y dareis, dad mas

Don Lorenzo Vander Hamen, Vicario de Juuiles.
Epistola al lector. He visto su *Politica* de v.m. con				220
la admiracion q. deuen los q. algo saben a sus
escritos. Dire con Ouidio, "Quid non laudabile vidi?"
o con n.ʳᵒ Biluilitano, "Quidquid calcas rossa," y q.
halle en ella vna bien deseada y alta materia del estado
xpiano en seruicio de ambas magestades, diuina y				225
humana, comercio de principes y exemplo de peca-
dores. Y q. le mando Dios a Josue q. no soltase el
libro de la ley de las manos si queria azertar a gouer-
nar. Josu. 1. 7.

219. MS: Juuides.
220. MS: Politica
221. A *d* appears under the first letter of 'admiracion.'
223. MS: Biuiliano (the reference is to Martial, who as a native of
Bilbilis, or Calatayud, was known as a "Bilbilitano").

APPENDIX II

BIBLIOGRAPHICAL DESCRIPTIONS

Abbreviations: B—Biblioteca, Bibliothèque, Bibliotek, etc. BN—Biblioteca Nacional, Bibliothèque Nationale, etc. Crosby—author's collection.

Microfilm of all MSS, of all copies of the Zaragoza editions, and of most copies of the other editions, is in my possession or in the Library of the University of Illinois. The particular copy on which each description is based appears first in each list of copies. The reference headings of the editions published in 1628, 1641 and 1647, which I have not seen, are in square brackets.

I. MANUSCRIPTS

Lost or Nonexistent Manuscripts

According to Luis Astrana Marín, there exists in the Biblioteca Nacional de Madrid a MS of the First Part of the *Política* (MS 18717, listed in Astrana, *Verso,* p. 1303b, no. 166, "Catálogo de Manuscritos"). Diligent search by the librarians at the Biblioteca Nacional has failed to uncover any such MS of the *Política;* MS 18717 itself contains historical material related to Philip III. Two MSS with similar numbers (MSS 18735 and 8719) are listed in the card catalogue of the Sala de Manuscritos as containing copies of the "Anotaciones a la *Política de Dios,*" an essay by Francisco Morovelli de Puebla, but again these two MSS contain no such material.

The Frías Manuscript

(author's collection)

Titlepage: Polytica de Dios. Gouierno de / Christo, y Tyrania de Satanas. / Escriuelo con las plumas de los Euange- / listas Don Françisco de Queuedo Ville- / gas, Cauallero del orden de Santia- / go, y Señor de la Villa de Juan / Abad. / Al [deleted: duque] Conde Duque, gran Canciller, / mi Señor, Don Gaspar de Guzman, Con / de de Oliuares, Sumiler de corps. / y cauallerico mayor de su Ma / gestad. / [A design] / Con licencia. / En Zaragoça por Pedro Verges a los señales. / año. 1625.

Colophon: none

Preliminaries: leaf 1r: titlepage. ll. 1v-2r: *Aprobación* by Esteban de Peralta, Zaragoza, Jan. 26, 1626. l. 2r-2v: *Licencia* by Juan de Salinas,

93

Zaragoza, Feb. 11, 1626. l. 3r-3v: Dedication to the Conde-duque, signed by Quevedo, in the Villa de Juan Abad, April 5, 1621. l. 4r: "A quien lee," signed by Quevedo. l. 4v: "El librero al lector," signed by Robert Duport, undated. ll. 5r-13r: Letter to Quevedo from Lorenzo Vander Hammen y León, undated. ll. 13v-14v: blank. Numbered pages 1-3: Quotations from Proverbs, vii, and Ecclesiastes, x; "Pregón y amenaza de la sabiduría," with quotations from Wisdom, vi and vii. pp. 3-5: "A los hombres que por el gran Dios de los exércitos tienen con título de reyes la tutela de las gentes: Pontífice, Emperador, Reyes, Príncipes." pp. 5-11: "En el gobierno superior de Dios sigue al entendimiento la voluntad."

Text: Twenty numbered chapters, pp. 12-220.

Table of Contents: Two leaves following p. 220.

Collation: [14]ff. + 1-220 pp. + [2]ff. Errors in pagination: p. 173 (numbered as 174), p. 174 (as 175), and thus in numerical order to p. 191, whose number is repeated on the next page in order to reestablish the correct pagination. Although the signatures are not marked with letters, the volume contains 16 signatures of eight leaves each (counting the two blank leaves before the titlepage, but not those after the last leaf of the table of contents). 10.4 × 14.7 cm.

Binding: Contemporary parchment, the covers reinforced with boards, the pages cut and gilded, and a few designs stamped in gold on the spine and at the corners of the covers. In the center of each cover, within an oval frame composed of tongues of fire, there is the gilded image of a crowned figure (God? the Virgin?) which bears in its arms a child (certainly Jesus Christ).

Source of the text: unknown, but the same source as for the first Zaragoza edition (see discussion in Chapter I).

Probable date: February, 1626 (see Chapter I).

Provenance: Library of the Duke of Frías (c. 1852; see Fernández-Guerra, *BAE* XXIII, p. cxiii, col. a, no. 1). From this library the MS passed to Fernández-Guerra himself, and then to his heir Luis Valdés. It is now the property of the present writer.

Bibliographical descriptions: Fernández-Guerra, *BAE* XXIII, p. cxiii, col. a, no. 1. Astrana, *Verso,* p. 1303b, no. 167 (an abbreviated copy of Fernández-Guerra's description).

The handwriting of the MS is relatively small: in general the letters measure between 0.15 and 0.2 cm. in height, not counting the ascenders and descenders, and in a page which measures 14.7 cm. in height, there will be between 20 and 23 lines, including running heads (one on each page) and catchwords. The handwriting seems to me to be similar to others which I have seen of the 17th century. I dare not assign a more precise date since I am not an expert in paleography, and have been unable to consult one. Fortunately, textual criticism offers more precise indications for the date of the MS. The handwriting seems to me to be uniform throughout the MS, which would suggest a single hand. The regularity and the clarity of the letters lead me to believe that the text was copied by a professional scribe (what is certain is that it cannot be Quevedo's autograph). As mentioned in Chapter I, Fernández-Guerra states that the handwritng is that of Quevedo's amanuensis, but he does not say how he knew this, nor who such an amanuensis may have been. In describing the MS of another of Quevedo's works, "La hora de todos y la fortuna con seso," Fernández-Guerra makes the same undocumented statement: "letra del amanuense de Quevedo" (*BAE* XXIII, p. cxvi). And although Fernández-Guerra does not say so, Astrana Marín says without explanation that the MS of "Su espada por Santiago" is an example of the "letra del amanuense de Quevedo" (*Verso,* p. 1313). I do not know the present location of the MS of "La hora de todos" (Astrana copied his description from Fernández-Guerra); an examination of the handwriting of "Su espada por Santiago" has convinced me that this MS and the MS of the *Política* were not copied by the same hand. I do not believe that anything certain is known about the identity of the copyist of this MS of the *Política.*

The MS Summary of the First Part of the Política

(Biblioteca Nacional de Madrid, MS 1092)

Title: Politica de Dios. Gouierno de Xpo / Tirania de Satanas. D. Fran^co Queuedo

Preliminaries (entire text): Pregon y amenaza de la Sauiduria fol. 1. / Pontifices emperadores, Reyes principes / A v^ro cuidado no a v^ro aluedrio os encomendo las gentes Dios Sapi / entia. 7. y os dio trabajo y afan honrosso no vanidad ni descanso

Text: Twenty numbered paragraphs, each summarizing one chapter of the Zaragoza version of the *Política.*

Epilogue: Don Lorenzo Vander Hamen, vicario de Juuides [sic]. Epístola al lector. [There follows in one paragraph a summary of the opening pages of Vander Hammen's letter, which appears in the preliminaries of all other known texts, and in them is addressed to Quevedo.]

Collation: the text occupies ff. 182r-185r of MS 1092 of the Biblioteca Nacional. 14.5 × 20.6 cm.

Handwriting: regular, small, and uniform throughout the MS. The handwriting seems to me to be similar to others which I have seen of the seventeenth century.

Source of the text: probably the first or second edition (Zaragoza, 1626), or one of the Pamplona editions (1626 and 1631). See discussion in Chapter IV.

Probable date: after 1629 (see Chapter IV).

Provenance: Biblioteca Real (Madrid).

Bibliographical description: José López de Toro and Ramón Paz Remolar, *Inventario general de manuscritos de la Biblioteca Nacional de Madrid* (Madrid, 1957), III, 305 (a general description of the entire volume which is MS 1092).

Rouen Manuscript

(Bibliothèque de la Ville de Rouen, MS Leber 894 [3094])

Titlepage: POLITICA DE / DIOS / *Gouierno de Christo / Tirania de Satanas / Escriuelo con las plumas de los Euangelis- / tas Don Francisco de Queuedo Villegas Caua- / llero de la Orden de Santiago, y Señor de la / Villa de Joan Abad. / Al Conde Duque, gran Canciller, mi se- / ñor, Don Gaspar de Guzman, Conde de Oli- / uares, Sumilier de Corps, y Cauallerizo / mayor de su Magestad / con lizencia en Barcelona / Por Esteuan libreros en la calle de S. Domingo / A costa de Lluch Durã, y Iacinto Argemir, Libreros*

Colophon: Con licencia en Barcelo- / na por Esteuan Libreros en / la Calle de S. Domingo, / Año M.DC.XXVI.

Preliminaries: Leaf 1r: titlepage. 1. 1v: blank. Folio 1r: *Aprobación y Licencia* by Tomás Roca and Francisco Terrè, Barcelona, June 30, 1626. ff. 1v-2v: *Aprobación* by Esteban de Peralta, Zaragoza, January 26. ff. 3r-3v: *Licencia* by Juan de Salinas, Zaragoza, February 11, 1626 and *Licencia* by Mendoza, Feb. 23, 1626. ff. 4r-5r: Dedication to Gaspar de Guzmán, Conde Duque de Olivares, signed by Quevedo, in the Villa de Juan Abad, April 5, 1621. f. 5v: "A quien lee," signed by Quevedo. ff. 6r-21r: Letter to Quevedo from Lorenzo Vander Hammen, undated. f. 21v: Quotations from Proverbs, vi and Ecclesiastes, x. ff. 22r-25v: "Pregón y amenaza de la Sabiduría," with translations from Wisdom, vi and vii. "A los hombres, que por el gran Dios de los exérçitos tienen con título de reyes la tutela de las gentes: Pontífice, Emperador, Reyes, Príncipes." ff. 25v-31v: "En el govierno superior de Dios sigue al entendimiento la voluntad."

Text: Twenty numbered chapters, ff. 31v-222v.

Table of Contents and Colophon: ff. 223r-225v.

Collation: [1]f. + 1-225 ff. No errors in foliation. 13.6 × 19.6 cm.

Binding: Parchment.

Handwriting: The MS is written in a large, regular and ornate set hand. Although such writing is difficult to analyze, and I am not an expert in paleography, it seems to me that in spite of the large size (generally considered typical of the eighteenth century), the hand shares several characteristics with others that I have seen assigned to the seventeenth century.

Source of the text: edition L (Barcelona, Esteban Liberòs, 1626).

Probable date: between 1626 and the end of the seventeenth century.

Provenance: Library of Jean Michel Constant Leber (1780-1859); sold in 1838 to the Bibliothèque de la Ville de Rouen.

Bibliographical descriptions: Catalogue des livres imprimés, manuscrits, estampes, dessins et cartes a jouer composant la Bibliothèque de M. C. Leber (Paris, 1839), I, 139, no. 894 (a brief reference). *Catalogue général des manuscrits des bibliothèques publiques de France* (Paris, 1888), II, 78 (a brief reference).

The Manuscript of the Second Part

(Real Academia de la Historia, Madrid;
Colección de Salazar y Castro, B-49)

Title: Politica de Dios Gouierno de christo / Tirania de Satanas / Por Don Fran.ᶜᵒ de Queuedo Villegas cau.º / de la orden de Santiago y s.ᵒʳ de la Villa de / la Torre de Juan Abad a nuestro santis.ᵐᵒ / P.ᵉ Vrbano octauo ob'po de Roma y / Pontifice Maximo

Colophon: none.

Preliminaries: f. 318r: title. ff. 318r-320v: Dedication to Pope Urban VIII, unsigned and undated. ff. 320v-322r: "A quien lee," unsigned and undated.

Text: eight numbered chapters, ff. 322r-395r, followed on f. 395v by the author's profession of loyalty to the Church and the King.

Collation: the MS occupies ff. 318r-395v of Codex B-49, Colección de Salazar y Castro, Real Academia de la Historia.

Source of the text: unknown.

Probable date: the seventeenth century, after 1635.

Provenance: Library of Luis de Salazar y Castro (c. 1700); Biblioteca de las Cortes (18th-19th centuries); Biblioteca de la Real Academia de la Historia, Madrid.

Bibliographical descriptions: Fernández-Guerra, ed. *Política de Dios,* by Quevedo (Madrid, 1868), II, xxi-xxiii, Prologue (a mere reference, with almost no descriptive material). Astrana, *Verso,* p. 1303b, no. 168 (a reference to the present location of the MS).

The handwriting of the MS presents several problems. Fernández-Guerra believed that this MS was a "copia mandada hacer a mi juicio por Quevedo en 1635" (ed. *Política de Dios,* by Quevedo, Madrid, 1868, Vol. II, p. xxii, "Prologue"). No reason is given for such a notion; perhaps it was the result of confusing the date of the composition of the first eight chapters, with the date on which the Academy MS may actually have been copied out. I know of no information which would support the idea that it was Quevedo himself who had this MS made.

Astrana Marín assigns the handwriting of this MS to the "segundo tercio del siglo XVII" (*Verso*, p. 1303b, 168), but such precise dating must be questioned when offered without documentation by one who is not an expert in paleography (further comments on Astrana's precision in dating handwriting may be seen in Juan Antonio Tamayo's excellent article, "El texto de los *Sueños*," *Boletín de la Biblioteca de Menéndez Pelayo*, XXI, 1945, p. 484).

In reality, I believe that the handwriting of this MS presents several problems which can only be solved by an expert paleographer. While making no pretense to such competence, I will describe such problems as I have found.

The text seems to have been copied by at least two different hands, the change occurring on f. 346v. Further but less striking variations, which may merely be due to different pens or different working conditions, seem to me to occur on ff. 318r, 328r, 328v, 334v, 341r, 344r, and 375v. And there are several folios which seem to bear one type of handwriting towards the top of the sheet and another towards the bottom, again perhaps nothing more than the result of working conditions: ff. 336r, 339r, 364v-366r, 374v, 376v, 378r, 379r, 379v.

Whatever the explanation of these apparent changes, it seems to me that all of the handwriting in the MS is similar to other examples which I have seen assigned to the seventeenth century.

II. Printed Editions

Edition X
(Zaragoza, 1626, First Edition)

Titlepage: POLITICA / DE DIOS. / GOVIERNO / DE CHRISTO: / TYRANIA DE / SATANAS. / *Escriuelo con las plumas de los Euangelistas, Don Fran-* / *cisco de Queuedo Villegas, Cauallero del Orden de* / *Santiago, y señor de la Villa de Iuan Abad.* / Al Conde Duque, gran Canciller, mi señor, Don / Gaspar de Guzman, Conde de Oliuares, / Sumilier de Corps, y Cauallerizo / mayor de su Magestad. / [A design] / CON LICENCIA. / [A line] / En Zaragoça: Por Pedro Verges: A los Señales. / Año M.DC.XXVI. / A costa de Roberto Duport, Mercader de Libros.

Colophon: Con licencia, en Çaragoça: Por Pedro / Verges. Año 1626.

Preliminaries: A1ʳ: titlepage. A1ᵛ: blank. A2ʳ: *Aprobación* by Esteban de Peralta, Zaragoza, Jan. 26, 1626. A2ᵛ: *Licencias* by Juan de Salinas, Zaragoza, Feb. 11, 1626, and Mendoza, Zaragoza, Feb. 23, 1626. A3ʳ: Dedication to Gaspar de Guzmán, Conde-duque de Olivares, signed by Quevedo, in the Villa de Juan Abad, April 5, 1621. A3ᵛ: "A quien lee," signed by Quevedo. A4ʳ: "El librero al lector," signed by Roberto

Duport. A4^v-B2^r: Letter to Quevedo from Lorenzo Vander Hammen, undated. B2^v, and numbered folios 1r-1v: Quotations from Proverbs, vi, and Ecclesiastes, x; "Pregón y amenaça de la sabiduría," with translations from Wisdom, vi and vii. Numbered folios 1v-2r: "A los hombres que por el gran Dios de los exércitos tienen con título de reyes la tutela de las gentes: Pontífice, Emperador, Reyes, Príncipes." ff. 2v-5r: "En el gouierno superior de Dios sigue al entendimiento la voluntad."

Text: Twenty numbered chapters, ff. 5r-81v.

Table of contents and colophon: 1 unnumbered folio.

Collation: [10] ff. + 1-81 ff. + [1] f. Errors in pagination: 26 (numbered as 20). Sigs. A-I^8, K-L^8, M^4. 9.3 × 14.6 cm.

Source of text: unknown, but the same as that of the Frías MS.

Bibliographical descriptions: none.

Copies: BN de Lisboa, B. da Ajuda (Lisbon), B. Universitaria de Sevilla. The titlepage and second leaf of the Seville copy are missing and in their place appears the titlepage of a copy of edition Q (Madrid, 1626). Between ff. 78v and 79r of the Seville copy there is inserted signature C (ff. 7r-14v), complete. Another copy of signature C appears in its proper place after f. 6v.

Edition Y

(Zaragoza, 1626, Second Edition)

Titlepage, colophon, preliminaries, text, and *table of contents* as in edition *X.*

Collation: as in edition X, but 9.9 × 15.1 cm.

Errors in foliation: f. 26 (numbered as 20 in all copies), ff. 51 as 50 and 53 as 52 (Illinois, Mazarine, Arsenal and Zaragoza copies), f. 69 as 6 (Madrid and Zaragoza copies), f. 74 as 7 (Illinois and Casanatense), and f. 81 as 8 (Illinois, Casanatense, Mazarine and Madrid). On the distribution of these errors, see Chapter II, sect. B.

Source of the text: edition X.

Bibliographical descriptions: Fernández-Guerra, *BAE* XXIII, p. xcii, col. a, no. 3; Astrana Marín, *Verso*, p. 1373b, no. 4 (an abbreviated copy of Fernández-Guerra); Manuel Jiménez Catalán, *Ensayo de una tipografía zaragozana del siglo XVII* (Zaragoza, 1927), pp. 153-154 (a detailed but not very accurate description of the copy in the University of Zaragoza). All of Fernández-Guerra's descriptions of printed editions were reprinted by Marcelino Menéndez y Pelayo in his unfinished *Obras completas de don Francisco de Quevedo Villegas* (Seville, 1897) I, 408 ff. (Bibliófilos Andaluces). Although it is impossible to be certain that Fernández-Guerra was describing the second rather than the first edition, the fact that the only copy of the latter now known to exist in Spain lacks a titlepage might mean that he saw only the second edition.

Copies: BN de Madrid, University of Illinois, B. Universitaria de Zaragoza, B. Casanatense (Rome), B. de l'Arsenal (Paris), B. Mazarine (Paris).

The more important textual and typographical differences between editions X and Y are discussed above in Chapter II, sect. B. The errors in foliation will serve for quick identification, as will the following three typographical details of the titlepage: 1) Line 2: the space between the word "Dios" and the period following it measures 1/24 inches (0.1 cm.) in X, but ⅛ inches (0.3 cm) in Y. 2) Line 13: the hook at the top of the letter *s* in the word "su" is missing in X; in Y the letter is perfect. 3) The right-hand end of the line across the titlepage (under the words "CON LICENCIA") ends in a bulb-like enlargement in X; in Y the line ends in a hook which points directly downward.

Edition Z

(Zaragoza, 1626, Third Zaragoza Edition)

Titlepage: POLITICA / DE DIOS, / GOVIERNO DE CHRISTO; / TIRANIA DE / SATANAS. / *ESCRIVELO CON LAS PLV-* / *mas de los Evangelistas, Don Francisco de Que-* / *vedo Villegas, Cavallero del Orden de/ Santiago, y Señor de la Villa de* / *Iuan Abad.* / AL CONDE DVQVE, GRAN / Canciller, mi señor, Don Gaspar de Guz- / man, Conde de Olivares, Sumiller de / Corps, y Cavallerizo Mayor de / su Magestad. / CON LICENCIA, / [A line] / En Zaragoça; Por Pedro Verges; a los Señales. / Año M.DC.XXVI. / *A costa de Roberto Duport, Mercader de libros.*

Colophon: None

Preliminaries: A1ʳ: titlepage. A1ᵛ: blank. A2ʳ: *Aprobación* by Esteban de Peralta, Zaragoza, Jan. 26, 1626. A2ᵛ: *Licencias* by Juan de Salinas, Zaragoza, Feb. 11, 1626, and Mendoza, Zaragoza, Feb. 23, 1626. A3ʳ: Dedication to Gaspar de Guzmán, Conde-duque de Olivares, signed by Quevedo, in the Villa de Juan Abad, April 5, 1621. A3ᵛ: "A quien lee," signed by Quevedo, and "El librero al lector," signed by Roberto Duport. A4ʳ-B2ᵛ: Letter to Quevedo from Lorenzo Vander Hammen, undated. B2ᵛ-B3ᵛ: Quotations from Proverbs, vi, and Ecclesiastes, x; and "Pregón y amenaza de la sabiduría," with translations from Wisdom, vi and vii. B3ᵛ-B4ʳ: "A los hombres que por el gran Dios de los exércitos tienen con título de reyes la tutela de las gentes: Pontífice, Emperador, Reyes, Príncipes." B4ʳ-B6ᵛ, and numbered folio 1r: "En el gouierno superior de Dios sigue al entendimiento la voluntad."

Text: Twenty numbered chapters, ff. 1r-77r.

Table of contents: ff. 77v-[78v].

Collation: [14] ff. + 1-77 ff. + [1] f. No errors in foliation. Sigs. A-I⁸, K-L⁸, M⁴. 9.6 × 15.2 cm.

Source of the text: edition Y.

Bibliographical description: There is a brief description in Antonio Palau y Dulcet, *Manual del librero hispanoamericano* (Barcelona, 1923), VI, 191. Palau believed that he was describing the first edition.

Copies: Harvard University Law Library, Boston Public Library (Ticknor Collection).

Edition P

(Pamplona, 1626)

Titlepage: POLITICA DE /DIOS. GOVIERNO / de Christo: Tirania de Sa- / tanas. / *Escriuelo con las plumas de los Euangelistas, Don / Francisco de Queuedo Villegas, Cauallero del / Orden de Santiago, y señor de la Villa / de Ioan Abad.* / Al Conde Duque, gran Canciller, mi señor, / Don Gaspar de Guzman, Conde de Oli- / uares, Sumilier de Corps, y Caualle- / rizo mayor de su Magestad. / [An escutcheon] / *Con licencia del Consejo Real: En Pamplona.* / [A line] / Por Carlos de Labàyen: Impressor del Reyno /de Nauarra. Año 1626.

Colophon: CON LICENCIA. / En Pamplona, por Carlos de La- / bayen: Impressor del Reyno / de Nauarra.

Preliminaries: A1ʳ: titlepage. A1ᵛ: blank. A2ʳ: *Aprobación* by Esteban de Peralta, Zaragoza, Jan. 26, 1626. A2ᵛ:*Licencias* by Juan de Salinas, Zaragoza, Feb. 11, 1626, and Mendoza, Zaragoza, Feb. 23, 1626. †1ʳ⁻ᵛ: *Tasa* by Martín de Uribarri, Pamplona, Oct. 6, 1626. †2ʳ: *Aprobación* by Pedro Ximénez, Pamplona, July 28, 1626. †2ᵛ: *Fe de erratas* by Pedro Ximénez, Pamplona, Oct. 2, 1626. A3ʳ: Dedication to Gaspar de Guzmán, Conde-Duque de Olivares, signed by Quevedo, in the Villa de Juan Abad, April 5, 1621. A3ᵛ: "A quien lee" signed by Quevedo. A4ʳ: "El librero al lector," signed by Roberto Duport. A4ᵛ-A8ᵛ, B1ʳ-B2ʳ: Letter to Quevedo from Lorenzo Vander Hammen, undated. B2ᵛ, numbered folio 1r-1v: Quotations from Proverbs, vi, and Ecclesiastes, x; "Pregón y amenaza de la sabiduría," with translations from Wisdom, vi and vii. Folios 1v-2r: "A los hombres que por el gran Dios de los exércitos tienen con título de reyes la tutela de las gentes: Pontífice, Emperador, Reyes, Príncipes." ff. 2v-5r: "En el gouierno superior de Dios sigue al entendimiento la voluntad."

Text: Twenty numbered chapters, ff. 5r-81v.

Table of contents and colophon: 1 unnumbered folio.

Collation: [12] ff. + 1-81 ff. + [1] f. Errors in foliation: ff. 26 (numbered

as 20), 51 (as 50), 53 (as 52), 79 (as 74). Sigs. A-I⁸, K-L⁸, M⁴. Signature
†² is inserted between leaves A2ᵛ and A3ʳ. Errors in numbering of signatures: F3 (as E3).

Source of the text: edition Y.

Bibliographical descriptions: Fernández-Guerra, *BAE* XXIII, p. xcii, col.
b, no. 5; Astrana, *Verso*, p. 1374a, no. 6; Antonio Pérez Goyena,
Ensayo de bibliografía navarra ([Burgos], 1947), I, p. 221, no. 396
(based on Fernández-Guerra).

Copies: BN de Madrid, BN de Paris.

Edition C

(Barcelona, Sebastián de Cormellas, 1626, First Barcelona Edition)

Titlepage: POLITICA / DE DIOS. / GOVIERNO DE / CHRISTO:
/ TYRANIA DE SATANAS. / *Escriuelo con las plumas de los
Euangelistas, Don Fran-* / *cisco de Queuedo Villegas, Cauallero del
Orden de San-* / *tiago, y señor de la Villa de Iuan Abad.* / Al Conde
Duque, gran Chanciller, mi señor, Don / Gaspar de Guzman, Conde
de Oliuares, Sumi- / lier de Corps, y Cauallerizo mayor / de su
Magestad. / Año [A design] 1626. / CON LICENCIA, / [A line] / En
Barcelona, Por Sebastian de Cormellas. / *Vendense en su misma casa
al Call.*

Colophon: Con licencia, en Barcelona en casa / Sebastian de Cormellas /
Año. 1626.

Preliminaries: A1ʳ: titlepage. A1ᵛ: blank. A2ʳ: *Aprobación* by Esteban
de Peralta, Zaragoza, Jan. 26, 1626. A2ᵛ: *Licencias* by Juan de
Salinas, Zaragoza, Feb. 11, 1626, and Mendoza, Zaragoza, Feb. 23,
1626. A3ʳ: Dedication to Gaspar de Guzmán, Conde-duque de Olivares, signed by Quevedo, in the Villa de Juan Abad, April 5, 1621.
A3ᵛ: "A quien lee," signed by Quevedo. A4ʳ: "El librero al lector,"
signed by Roberto Duport. A4ᵛ-B2ʳ: Letter to Quevedo from Lorenzo
Vander Hammen, undated. B2ᵛ, and numbered folio 1ʳ: Quotations
from Proverbs, vi, and Ecclesiastes, x. "Pregón y amenaça de la sabiduría," with translations from Wisdom, vi and vii. f. 1r-1v: "A los
hombres que por el gran Dios de los exércitos tienen con título de
reyes la tutela de las gentes: Pontífice, Emperador, Reyes, Príncipes."
f. 2r-3v: "En el gouierno superior de Dios sigue al entendimiento la
voluntad."

Text: Twenty numbered chapters, ff. 4r-64v.

Table of contents and colophon: 2 unnumbered folios.

Collation: [10] ff. + 1-64 ff. + [2] ff. Sigs. A-I⁸, K⁴. No errors in foliation. 10.5 × 15.0 cm.

Source of the text: edition Y.

Bibliographical descriptions: Fernández-Guerra, *BAE* XXIII, p. xcii, col. b, no. 4; Astrana, *Verso,* p. 1374a, no. 5.

Copies: Crosby, BN Centrale (Florence), B. Apostolica Vaticana (Rome).

Edition L

(Barcelona, Esteban Liberòs, 1626, Second Barcelona Edition)

Titlepage: POLITICA / DE DIOS. / GOVIERNO DE CHRISTO, / TIRANIA DE SATANAS. / *Escriuelo con las plumas de los Euangelistas, Don Fran-* / *cisco de Queuedo Villegas, Cauallero del Orden de* / *Santiago, y señor de la Villa de Iuan Abad.* / Al conde Duque, gran Canciller, mi señor Don Gas- / par de Guzman, Conde de Oliuares, Sumilier de / Corps, y Cauallerizo mayor de su Magestad. / Año [A portrait of Christ in regal robes, with the legend: "IESVS XPS."] 1626. / *Con Licencia en Barcelona.* / [A line] / Por Esteuan Liberos en la Calle de Santo Domingo. / *A costa de Lluch Duran y Yacinto Argemir Libreros.*

Colophon: Con Licencia: En Barcelona por Esteuan / Liberòs en la Calle de S. Domingo. / Año M.DC.XXVI.

Preliminaries: A1^r: titlepage. A1^v: blank. A2^r: *Aprobación y Licencia* by Tomás Roca and Francisco Terré, Barcelona, June 30, 1626. A2^v: *Aprobación* by Esteban de Peralta, Zaragoza, Jan. 26, 1626. A3^r: *Licencia* by Juan de Salinas, Zaragoza, Feb. 11, 1626 and *Licencia* by Mendoza, Zaragoza, Feb. 23, 1626. A3^v: Dedication to Gaspar de Guzmán, Conde Duque de Olivares, signed by Quevedo, in the Villa de Juan Abad, April 5, 1621. A4^r: "A quien lee," signed by Quevedo. A4^v-B2^v: Letter to Quevedo from Lorenzo Vander Hammen, undated. B2^v: Quotations from Proverbs, vi, and Ecclesiastes, x. Folios 1r-2r: "Pregón y amenaça de la sabiduría," with translations from Wisdom, vi and vii. "A los hombres que por el gran Dios de los exércitos tienen con título de reyes la tutela de las gentes: Pontífice, Emperador, Reyes, Príncipes." ff. 2v-4v: "En el gouierno superior de Dios sigue al entendimiento la voluntad."

Text: Twenty numbered chapters, ff. 4v-69v.

Table of contents and colophon: 1 unnumbered folio.

Collation: [10] ff. + 1-69 ff. + [1] f. Errors in foliation: f. 5 (unnumbered); f. 69 (numbered as 70). Sigs. A-I^8, K^8. 9.9 × 14.4 cm.

Source of the text: edition C.

Bibliographical descriptions: Fernández-Guerra, *BAE* XXIII, p. xcii, col. b, no. 6; Astrana, *Verso,* p. 1374a, no. 7.

Copies: BN de Paris, British Museum (London), B. Governativa (Cremona), B. Universitaria Alessandrina (Rome).

Appendix II

Edition M

(Milan, 1626)

Titlepage: POLITICA / DE DIOS. / GOVIERNO DE CHRISTO, / TIRANIA DE SATANAS. / *Escriuelo con las plumas de los Euange-listas,* / *Don Francisco de Queuedo Villegas, Caua-* / *llero del Orden de Santiago, y señor de la* / *Villa de Iuan Abad.* / Al Conde Duque, gran Canciller, mi señor, / DON GASPAR DE GVZMAN, / Conde de Oliuares, Sumilier de Corps, y / Cauallerizo mayor de su Magestad. / [A picture of a feline animal within a design] / EN MILAN, / [A line] / Por Iuan Baptista Bidelo, Año 1626.

Colophon: None.

Preliminaries: page [1]: titlepage. p. [2]: "Imprimatur [¶] F. Vinc. Aquens. Prouic. S. Officij Med. [¶] Fr. Al. Bariola Consultor S. Offitij pro Illustriss. D. Card. Archiep. [¶] Vidit Saccus pro Excellentiss. Senatu." p. 3: *Aprobación y Licencia* by Tomás Roca, Barcelona, June 30, 1626. p. 4-5: *Aprobación* by Esteban de Peralta, Zaragoza, Jan. 26, 1626. p. 6: *Licencias* by Juan de Salinas, Zaragoza, Feb. 11, 1626, and Mendoza, Zaragoza, Feb. 23, 1626. pp. 7-8: Dedication to Gaspar de Guzmán, Conde-duque de Olivares, signed by Quevedo in the Villa de Juan Abad, April 5, 1621. p. 9: "A quien lee," signed by Quevedo. pp. 10-23: Letter to Quevedo from Lorenzo Vander Hammen, undated, followed by Quotations from Proverbs, vi, and Ecclesiastes, x. pp. 24-27: "Pregón y amenaça de la sabiduría," with translations from Wisdom, vi and vii; and "A los hombres que por el gran Dios de los exércitos tienen con título de reyes la tutela de las gentes: Pontífice, Emperador, Reyes, Príncipes." pp. 27-32: "En el gouierno superior de Dios sigue al entendimiento la voluntad."

Text: Twenty numbered chapters, pp. 32-173.

Table of contents: 4 unnumbered pages immediately following p. 173.

Collation: [1] f. + 3-173 pp. + [2] ff. Sigs. A-G^{12}, H^5. 8.0 × 13.4 cm.

Source of the text: edition L.

Bibliographical descriptions: Astrana, *Verso,* p. 1374b, no. 8; Eduart Toda y Güell, *Bibliografia espanyola d'Italia* (Castell de Sant Miquel d'Escornalbou [Barcelona], 1929), III, p. 392, no. 4095 (no one has seen the copy which Toda y Güell states is in the BN de Madrid).

Copies: Crosby, Staatsbibliothek (Munich), BN Centrale (Florence), B. Ambrosiana (Milan), B. Governativa (Cremona).

Edition Q

(Madrid, 1626, First Authorized Edition)

Titlepage: POLITICA DE / DIOS. GOVIERNO DE / CHRISTO. / *AVTOR DON FRANCISCO DE* / *Queuedo Villegas, Cauallero de la*

*Orden de / Santiago, señor de la villa de la Torre / de Iuan Abad. / A
DON GASPAR DE GVZMAN / Conde Duque, gran Canciller / mi
señor. / LLEVA AÑADIDOS TRES CAPITVLOS / que le faltauan, y
algunas planas, y renglones, y va / restituìdo a la verdad de su / original. /* Paul. I. Cor. 3. *Vnusquisque autem videat quomodo / super
aedificet, fundamentum enim aliud nemo potest / ponere praeter id
quod positum est, quod est /* CHRISTVS IESVS. / Ioan. capit. 13. *Exemplum enim dedi vobis, vt / quemadmodum ego seu vobis, ita & / vos
faciatis. /* Año [A small design] 1626 / *CON PRIVILEGIO* / [A line]
/ En Madrid, *Por la viuda de Alonso Martin.* / A costa de Alonso
Perez mercader de libros.

Colophon: None.

Preliminaries: ¶1ʳ: titlepage. ¶1ᵛ: blank. ¶2ʳ-2ᵛ: Dedication to Gaspar
de Guzmán, unsigned and undated. ¶3ʳ: *Suma del priuilegio* by
Sebastián de Contreras, Madrid, Oct. 1, 1626. *Suma de tasa,* signed
by Fernando de Vallejo, Nov. 11, 1626. *Fe de erratas,* signed by
Murcia de la Llana, Madrid, Oct. 5, 1626. ¶3ʳ: *Aprobación* by M. Gil
González de Avila, Madrid, Sept. 16, 1626. ¶4ʳ-4ᵛ: *Aprobación* by
Fray Cristóbal de Torres, Madrid, Aug. 27, 1626. ¶5ʳ-5ᵛ: *Aprobación*
by P. Pedro de Urteaga, undated. ¶6ʳ-6ᵛ: *Aprobación* by Padre Gabriel
de Castilla, undated. ¶7ʳ-¶¶5ᵛ: Letter to Quevedo from Lorenzo Vander
Hammen, undated. ¶¶6ʳ-¶¶7ᵛ: Quotations from Proverbs, vi, and
Ecclesiastes, x. "Pregón y amenaça de la sabiduría," with translations
from Wisdom, vi and vii. "A los hombres, que por el gran Dios de los
exércitos tienen con título de Reyes la tutela de las gentes: Pontífice,
Emperador, Reyes, Príncipes." ¶¶8ʳ-¶¶¶1ᵛ: "A los doctores sin luz que
muerden y no leen," unsigned, but by Quevedo. ¶¶¶2ʳ-¶¶¶4ᵛ: "A Don
Felipe Quarto, nuestro señor," signed by Quevedo, undated.

Text: Twenty-four numbered chapters, ff. 1r-98r, followed on f. 98v by
"A quien lee," signed by Quevedo.

Table of contents: 2 unnumbered folios.

Collation: [20] ff. + 1-98 ff. + [2] ff. Errors in foliation: 62 (numbered as
64), 64 (as 62). Sigs. ¶-¶¶⁸, ¶¶¶⁴, A-I⁸, K-M⁸, N⁴. 9.5 × 14 cm.

Source of the text: edition Y.

Bibliographical descriptions: Fernández-Guerra, *BAE* XXIII, p. xcii, col.
b, no. 7; Astrana, *Verso,* p. 1374b, no. 9.

Copies: BN de Madrid, B del Monasterio del Escorial, Crosby (engraving), Crosby (Fernández-Guerra). The titlepage alone of a lost copy
appears in the Seville copy of edition X (see above).

The Crosby (Fernández-Guerra) copy was once owned by Aureliano
Fernández-Guerra (it contains his stamp on the flyleaves, and apparently
came from the library of his heir, Luis Valdés). Although the titlepage
and folios [7r-17v] are missing, this copy is interesting because it contains

Fernández-Guerra's pencil-marks in the margins of many pages. These simple lines indicate the passages he found difficult to understand, and those which he emended silently in his editions.

The Crosby (engraving) copy is the only known copy which contains an engraving on folio [2r] above the dedication to the Count-Duke of Olivares. This engraving depicts a hill surmounted by an ark to which a white dove with an olive branch in its beak is flying. Below the dove a raven flies or drops downward towards a tree growing at the base of the hill. Near the two birds is the legend "oliva columbae non coruo" ("the olive branch for the dove, not the crow"), and in the double border of the engraving, PHILLIPVS RAMO FOELICIS OLIVAE LVSTRAVIT Q̄, VIROS NON VIRVS. In this last legend, 'Philippus' refers of course to King Philip IV, and 'ramus olivae' to the Count-Duke of Olivares, which probably means that 'lustravit' should be understood in its primitive sense of 'purified.' But the text of the rest of the legend is difficult to interpret, if not actually corrupt (the misspelling of 'Philippus' suggests an ignorant engraver, who may well have made one or more errors in transcribing the final words). There is obviously a pun involved in the parallel construction of 'viros' and 'virus,' and both could be accusative as direct objects of 'lustravit.' But to translate the legend as "Philip with the branch of the fortunate olive tree purified men, not poison," would be to ignore the puzzling 'Q̄', which in the engraving appears clearly as transcribed above. It may even be that 'Q̄' represents an ignorant engraver's hispanized abbreviation or emendation.

The Crosby (engraving) copy also contains corrections of two errors found in all other copies: on the title page, the word 'seu' is corrected to 'feci' in the phrase "quemadmodum ego feci vobis, ita vos faciatis," and on f. 27v, the word 'morta' at the end of a line is corrected to 'mortal.' Since close comparison of all the signatures of the four copies of edition Q shows that all were printed from the same forms, the engraving copy must contain signatures which were corrected in the course of impression.

Edition R

(Madrid, 1626, Second Authorized Edition)

Titlepage: POLITICA DE / DIOS. GOVIERNO DE / CHRISTO. / *AVTOR DON FRANCISCO DE / Queuedo Villegas, Cauallero de la Orden de / Santiago, señor de la villa de la Torre / de Iuan Abad. /* A DON GASPAR DE GVZMAN / Conde Duque, gran Canciller / mi señor. / *LLEVA AÑADIDOS TRES CAPITVLOS / que le faltauan, y algunas planas, y renglones, y va / restituido a la verdad de su / original. /* Paulo I. Cor. 3. *Vnusquisque autē videat quomodo /*

super aedificet, fundamentum enim aliud nemo potest / ponere praeter id quod positum est, quod est. / CHRISTVS IESVS. */* Ioan. cap. 13. *Exemplum enim dedi vobis, vt quemadmodum / ego, seu vobis, ita & vos faciatis. /* Año [A small design] 1626. */ CON PRIVILEGIO. /* [A line] / En Madrid, *Por la viuda de Alonso Martin.* / A costa de Alonso Perez mercader de libros.

Colophon, preliminaries, text and *collation* as in edition Q.

Errors in foliation: f. 12 (numbered as 21), f. 53 (as 52), f. 62 (as 64), f. 64 (as 62), f. 82 (87), f. 87 (78), f. 92 (93). Sigs. as in edition Q, except that ¶2 is unnumbered, and ¶3 is numbered A3. 9 × 14.2 cm.

Source of text: edition Q.

Bibliographical descriptions: none.

Copies: BN de Lisboa.

The margins of the unique copy of R contain numerous MS notes in Portuguese, in a hand similar to seventeenth-century Spanish examples. The word 'seu' on the titlepage has been corrected by hand to 'feci' (see the engraving copy of edition Q).

[Madrid, 1628]

Titlepage: presumably similar to the titlepage of edition S (Salamanca, 1629). Possibly published by Pedro Tazo (see below).

Preliminaries: Aprobaciones by Miguel Sánchez, Madrid, Sept. 4, 1627, and Juan de Jáuregui, Madrid, Sept. 26, 1627. *Privilegio,* by Pedro de Contreras, Madrid, Nov. 28, 1627. *Tasa* by Hernando de Vallejo, Madrid, Jan. 24, 1628. The preliminary articles written by Quevedo were presumably those found in the Zaragoza version of the *Política.*

Text: Twenty numbered chapters.

Collation: 14 signatures.

Source of the text: edition Y (2nd Zaragoza, 1626).

Bibliographical descriptions: none.

Copies: none known to the present writer.

As mentioned in Chapter V, the source of information about this edition is the edition published at Salamanca in 1629, which contains preliminary material clearly taken from an edition published at Madrid in 1628. Although the Salamanca edition does not supply the name of the printer of the Madrid edition, it is possible that when Juan Pérez de Montalbán mentioned an edition published in Madrid between 1627 and 1632 by Pedro Tazo, he was referring to the edition of 1628 ("Indice de los ingenios de Madrid," in *Para todos,* Pamplona, 1702, p. 519—first edition. Madrid, 1632).

Edition S

(Salamanca, 1629)

Titlepage: POLITICA DE / Dios, gouierno de / Christo, y tirania de / Satanas. / *Escriuelo con las plumas de los / Euangelistas D. Francisco / de Queuedo Villegas Caua- / llero de la Orden de Santia- / go y Señor de la villa de Iuan / Abad.* / Dirigido al Duque Conde./ CON LICENCIA. / En Salamanca, por Iuan Fer- / nandez. año M.DC. XXIX.

Colophon: None.

Preliminaries: a1^r: titlepage. a1^v: blank. a2^r-a3^r: Dedication to Gaspar de Guzmán, Conde [sic] de Olivares, signed by Quevedo, in the Villa de Juan Abad, April 5, 1628 [sic]. a3^v-a6^v: *Privilegio* by Pedro de Contreras, Madrid, Nov. 28, 1627. e1^r-e1^v: *Tasa* by Hernando de Vallejo, Madrid, Jan. 24, 1628. e2^r-e3^r: *Aprobaciones* by Miguel Sánchez, Madrid, Sept. 4, 1627, and Juan de Jáuregui, Madrid, Sept. 26, 1627. e3^v-e4^r: Quotations from Proverbs, vi, and Ecclesiastes, x. e4^r-e5^v: "Pregón y amenaza de la sabiduría," with translations from Wisdom, vi and vii. e5^v-i1^r: "A los hombres que por el gran Dios de los exércitos tienen con título de Reyes la tutela de las gentes como. [¶] Pontífice, Emperado [sic], Rey, Príncipes, soberanos, Monarc." i1^r-i6^v: "En el gouierno superior de Dios sigue al entendimiento la voluntad." i6^v: *Fe de Erratas.*

Text: Twenty numbered chapters, pp. 1-321.

Table of contents: 3 unnumbered pages immediately following p. 321.

Collation: [18] ff. + 1-321 pp. + [3] pp. Errors in pagination: pp. 60 (numbered as 68), 174 (178), 175 (176), 240 (204), 307 (387). Sigs. a-e-i^6, A-I^6, K-T^6, V-Z^6, Aa-Dd^6. Errors in signatures: e3 (numbered as e4), i3 (as i4). 9.0 × 14.6 cm.

Source of the text: lost edition of Madrid, 1628.

Bibliographical descriptions: none.

Copies: Crosby, BN de Paris.

Barcelona, 1629

Titlepage: POLITICA / DE DIOS, / GOVIERNO DE CHRISTO, / TIRANIA DE SATANAS. / *Escriuelo con las plumas de los Euangelistas, don / Francisco de Queuedo Villegas, Cauallero del / Orden de Santiago, y señor de la / Villa de Iuan Abad.* / Al Conde Duque, gran Canciller, mi señor, don / Gaspar de Guzman, Conde de Oliuares, Sumi- / lier de Corps, y Cauallerizo mayor / de su Magestad. / Año [A design] 1629 / *Con Licencia en Barcelona,* / [A line] / Por PEDRO LACAVALLERIA, en la Calle / de Arlet, tjunto [sic] la Libreria.

Colophon: Con licencia, en Barcelona, por PE- / DRO LACAVA-LLERIA, en la Calle / de Arlet, junto la Libreria, / Año 1629.
Preliminaries: A1^r: titlepage. A1^v: blank. A2^r: *Aprobación y Licencia* by Tomás Roca, Barcelona, Jun. 30, 1626. A2^v: *Aprobación* by Esteban de Peralta, Zaragoza, Jan. 26, 1626. A3^r: *Licencias* by Juan de Salinas, Zaragoza, Feb. 11, 1626, and Mendoza, Zaragoza, Feb. 23, 1626. A3^v: Dedication to Gaspar de Guzmán, Conde [sic] de Olivares, signed by Quevedo, in the Villa de Juan Abad, April 5, 1621. A4^r: "A quien lee," signed by Quevedo. A4^v-folio 1r: Letter to Quevedo from Lorenzo Vander Hammen, undated, and Quotations from Proverbs, vi, and Ecclesiastes, x. ff. 1v-2r: "Pregón y amenaça de la sabiduría," with translations from Wisdom, vi and vii. ff. 2r-2v: "A los hombres que por el gran Dios de los exércitos tienen con título de reyes la tutela de las gentes: Pontífice, Emperador, Reyes, Príncipes." ff. 2v-4v: "En el gouierno superior de Dios sigue al entendimiento la voluntad."
Text: Twenty numbered chapters, ff. 4v-64v.
Table of contents and colophon: 3 unnumbered folios.
Collation: [9] ff. + 1-64 ff. + [3] ff. Error in foliation: f. 6 (numbered as 7). Sigs. A-I^8, R^4.
Source of the text: edition L (Barcelona, Liberòs, 1626).
Bibliographical descriptions: Fernández-Guerra, *BAE* XXIII, p. xciv, col. a, no. 24; Astrana, *Verso*, p. 1378a, no. 29.
Copies: BN de Madrid (two copies: R/5909 and U/1007), BN Centrale (Florence), B. Apostolica Vaticana, Niedersächsische Staats- und Universitätsbibliothek (Göttingen).

Lisbon, 1630

Titlepage: POLITICA DE / DIOS, GOVIERNO DE / CHRISTO. / *AVTOR DON FRANCISCO DE / Queuedo Villegas, Cauallero del Orden de / Santiago, señor de la villa de la / Torre de Iuan Abad. / A DON GASPAR DE GVZMAN / Conde Duque, gran Canciller / mi señor. / LLEVA AÑADIDOS TRES CAPI- / tulos que le faltauan, y algunas planas, y / renglones, y va restituido a la ver- / dad de su original. /* Paulo I. Cor. 3 *Vnusquisque autem videat quomodo / super aedificiet* [sic] *fundamentum enim aliud nemo potest / ponere praeter id quod positum est, quod est* / CHISTVS [sic] IESVS. / Ioan cap. 13. *Exemplum enim dedi vobis, vt quem- / admodum, ego feci vobis ita et vos faciatis.* / Año [A design] 1630. / [A line] / *CON LICENCIA.* / EM LISBOA. Por Mathias Rodrigues. / *A costa de Domingos Pedroso Mercader de libros.*
Colophon: None. Folio 90v: "A quien lee," signed by Quevedo.
Preliminaries: A1^r: titlepage. A1^v: blank. A2^r: *Licencia* by Ayres Correa,

Lisboa, Nov. 15, 1629. A2^v: *Licencias* by G. Pereira, Francisco Barreto, Juan da Silva and Antonio de Sousa, Lisboa, Nov. 16, 1629, by Gaspar do Rego de Afonseca, Lisboa, Dec. 6, 1629, by Pimenta d'Abreu and Barreto, Lisboa, Dec. 7, 1629, and by Ayres Correa, Lisboa, Jan. 13, 1630, and *Tasa*. A3^r: Dedication to Gaspar de Guzmán, Conde [sic] de Olivares, signed by Quevedo, in the Villa de Juan Abad, April 5, 1621. A3^v: "Al lector," signed by Quevedo. A4^r-B2^v: Letter to Quevedo from Lorenzo Vander Hammen, undated. B2^v-B3^r: Quotations from Proverbs, vi, and Ecclesiastes, x; "Pregón y amenaza de la sabiduría," with translations from Wisdom, vi and vii. B3^v-B4^r: "A los hombres que por el gran Dios de los exércitos tienen con título de reyes la tutela de las gentes: Pontífice, Emperador, Reyes, Príncipes." B4^r-B6^v, and folio 1r: "En el gouierno superior de Dios sigue al entendimiento la voluntad."

Text: Twenty-three numbered chapters, ff. 1r-90r.

Table of contents: 2 unnumbered folios.

Collation: [14] ff. + 1-90 ff. + [2] ff. Errors in foliation: ff. 3 (numbered as 4), 14 (as 15), 16 (as 61), 42 (24), 44-88 (as 46-90), 80 (79), 81 (80), 82 (81). Sigs. A-I^8, K-N^8. Errors in signatures: M5 (numbered as M4).

Source of the text: titlepage and chapters XI, XII and XIII are from edition R (2nd Madrid, 1626); all preliminaries and remaining text are from edition Z (3rd Zaragoza, 1626).

Bibliographical descriptions: Astrana, *Verso*, p. 1380a, no. 45.

Copies: BN de Madrid (two copies: R/4724 and R/12039), BN de Lisboa, B. Pública Municipal (Porto, Portugal), Cambridge University Library (England), Library of Congress (Washington, D.C.), Library of the University of Pennsylvania (Philadelphia, U.S.A.).

Pamplona, 1631

Titlepage: POLITICA DE / DIOS, GOVIERNO / de Christo: Tirania de Sa- / tanas. / *Escriuelo con las plumas de los Euangelistas, Don Fran- / cisco de Queuedo Villegas, Cauallero del Orden de / Santiago, y señor de la Villa de Ioan / Abad.* / Al Conde Duque, gran Canciller, mi señor, Don Gas- / par de Guzman, Conde de Oliuares, Sumilier de / Corps, y Cauallerizo mayor de su Magestad. / *Añadidos a este Tratado.* / [A vertical line in the center of the page separates the following numbers: 1 and 2, on the left, from 3 and 4, on the right:] 1. La Historia del Bus- / con. / 2. Los sueños. / 3. Discurso de todos los dañados, y malos. / 4. Cuento de Cuentos. / [A design] / *Con licencia del Consejo Real:* / *En Pamplona.* / [A line] / Por Carlos de Lavàyen: Impressor del Reyno de / Nauarra. Año 1631.

Colophon: None.

Preliminaries: A1^r: titlepage. A1^v: blank. A2^r-A2^v: *Tasa* by Martín de Uribarri, Pamplona, Oct. 6, 1626. A3^r: *Aprobación* by Pedro Jiménez, Pamplona, July 28, 1626. A3^v: *Fe de Erratas* by Pedro Jiménez, Pamplona, Oct. 2, 1626. A4^r: *Aprobación* by Esteban de Peralta, Zaragoza, Jan. 26, 1626. A4^v: *Licencias* by Juan de Salinas, Zaragoza, Feb. 11, 1626, and Mendoza, Zaragoza, Feb. 23, 1626. A5^r: Dedication to Gaspar de Guzmán, Conde [sic] de Olivares, signed by Quevedo, in the Villa de Juan Abad, April 5, 1621. A5^v: "A quien lee," signed by Quevedo. A6^r: "El librero al lector," signed by Roberto Duport. A6^v-B6^r: Letter to Quevedo from Lorenzo Vander Hammen, undated, and Quotations from Proverbs, vi and Ecclesiastes, x. B6^v-folio 1v: "Pregón y amenaça de la sabiduría," with quotations from Wisdom, vi and vii. ff. 1v-2r: "A los hombres que por el gran Dios de los exércitos tienen con título de reyes la tutela de las gentes: Pontífice, Emperador, Reyes, Príncipes." ff. 2r-5r: "En el gouierno superior de Dios sigue al entendimiento la voluntad."

Text: Twenty numbered chapters, ff. 5r-81v.
Collation: [14] ff. + 1-81 ff. Sigs. A-I^8, K-L^8, M^7.
Source of the text: edition P (Pamplona, 1626).
Bibliographical descriptions: Fernández-Guerra, *BAE* XXIII, p. xcv, col. a, no. 36; Astrana, *Verso*, p. 1381a, no. 50; Antonio Pérez Goyena, *Ensayo de bibliografía navarra* ([Burgos], 1947), I, p. 263, no. 432.
Copies: BN de Madrid (two copies: R/12910 and R/13367), BN de Lisboa, B. Mazarine (Paris), B. de L'Arsenal (Paris), B. Municipale de Rouen, B. Municipale de Troyes, B. Publique de Nancy, B. Casanatense (Rome), State M.E. Saltykov-Shcheredrin Public Library (Leningrad), B. der Rijksuniversitect te Leiden (Netherlands), Österreichische Nationalbibliothek (Vienna), Kongelige B. (Copenhagen), Bayerische Staatsbibliothek (Munich), Bodleian Library (Oxford), British Museum (London), Library of Congress (Washington, D.C.), Newberry Library (Chicago), Library of the University of Pennsylvania (Philadelphia).

[Madrid, 1641]

This edition, of which no known copy or other description exists, is described as follows by Astrana (*Verso*, p. 1387b, no. 89):

"Politica de dios, govierno de Christo, tirania de Satanás. / Escrivelo con las plumas de los Evangelistas, don Francisco de Quevedo Villegas, cauallero de la orden de Santiago y señor de la villa de Juan Abad. / Al conde duque, gran canciller &. / En Madrid, por Juan Sanchez, año de 1641. / (En 8.°)"

The presence of the words "tiranía de Satanás" in the title would indicate that the text followed the early Zaragoza version.

[Warsaw, 1647]

This edition, of which no copy is known to exist, has been described as follows by Fernández-Guerra (*BAE* XXIII, p. xcvii, col. c, no. 68): "Politica de Dios y Govierno de Christo. ¶Por Don Francisco de Queuedo Villegas, Cauallero de la Orden de Santiago, señor de la Villa de la Torre de Iuan Abad. Varsoviae, In Officina Petri Elert S. R. M. Typographi, Anno Domini, 1647 (En 8.°)"

The title, if correctly transcribed, indicates that the text followed the revised version (the words "tiranía de Satanás" are missing), and was probably made from one of the two editions published in Madrid in 1626. As mentioned above in Chapter V, it is most likely that this edition was printed in Latin or Spanish, rather than Polish.

Edition B

(Madrid, 1648, First 1648 edition)

Titlepage: ENSEÑANZA ENTRETENIDA, / I / DONAIROSA MO-RALIDAD, / Comprehendida / *En el Archivo ingenioso de las Obras* / *escritas en Prosa,* / DE DON FRANCISCO DE QVEVEDO VILLEGAS, / CABALLERO DE LA ORDEN DE SANTIAGO, / I SEÑOR DE LA VILLA DE LA TORRE DE IVAN ABAD. / *Contienense juntas en este Tomo, las que sparcidas en diffe-* / *rentes Libros* *hasta ahora se han* / *impresso.* / [A design] / EN MADRID, / Lo imprimio EN SV OFFICINA DIEGO DIAZ / DE LA CARRERA, / [A line] / Año M.DC. XLVIII. / *A costa de Pedro Coello Mercader* / *de* *Libros.*

Colophon: None.

Preliminaries: leaf 1r: titlepage. ll. 1v-2r: blank. 1. 2v: an escutcheon. l. 3r-3v: Dedication to Pedro Pacheco Girón, signed by Pedro Coello, undated. l. 4r: *Aprobaciones,* by Diego del Carpio and Juan Vélez Zabala. *Suma de la Licencia* by José de Arteaga, May 6, 1648. *Tasa* by José Arteaga, Madrid, June 22, 1648. *Erratas* by Carlos Murcia de la Llana, Madrid, June 20, 1648. l. 4v: Table of contents.

Text of the *Política de Dios,* Part I: twenty-four chapters, pp. 259-329, with neither preliminaries nor title (in the table of contents the title is listed as "Govierno superior de Dios, i Tirania de Satanas," which is a combination of the title of the first chapter and the title of the Zaragoza version).

Collation: [4] ff. + 1-396 pp. Errors in pagination: 25 (numbered as 24), 221-225 (as 215-219), 239 (as 236). Sigs.: [undesignated]⁴, A-I⁸, K-T⁸, V-Y⁸, Z⁴, Aa-Bb⁸, Cc⁶. 15.4 × 20.5 cm.

Source of the text of the *Política:* edition Q (1st Madrid, 1626).

Bibliographical descriptions: Fernández-Guerra, *BAE* XXIII, p. xcviii, col. a, no. 71; Astrana, *Verso,* p. 1389b; no. 99; Amédée Mas, ed. Quevedo, *Las zahurdas de Plutón* (*El sueño del Infierno*), (Poitiers, [1956]), p. 27b, "Étude bibliografique." None of these descriptions of the titlepage of the Madrid copy is entirely accurate.

Copies: Crosby (Gigas), Crosby (Ramírez de Arellano), BN de Madrid, B. Central (Barcelona). "Gigas" refers to the library stamp of Emil Gigas on the flyleaf of that copy, and "Ramírez de Arellano" to the signature of Juan Ramírez de Arellano on the titlepage of the other copy. There seems to be no way of knowing which of the many nobles named Juan Ramírez de Arellano once owned the latter copy. Another copy of this edition is listed in the Note on p. 118.

In the various copies of this edition there are three groups of bibliographical characteristics which require further discussion: the lack of three leaves in the Barcelona copy, the two printings of the preliminaries of the edition, and the changes effected in signature X.

The Barcelona copy lacks leaf 2, which in the Madrid and Crosby copies contains an engraving of the coat of arms of Pedro Pacheco Girón, and it also lacks pages 393-396 (the last two leaves in the book). Because the binding of this copy is very weak, it may well be that when printed, the volume contained these leaves, which were subsequently lost. (The engraving was omitted from the second 1648 edition, for the numbering of the signatures in that edition shows that nothing has been lost from the only extant copy.) With respect to the last two missing leaves of the Barcelona copy, the lower right-hand corner of the leaf immediately preceding them is torn, and there is thus no way of knowing whether or not it ever contained a catchword. But the recto of this leaf contains the signature mark "Cc3," which would indicate that the signature was printed in sixes (had it been in fours, the third leaf would not have borne any mark). Thus it seems that the Barcelona copy originally contained the three leaves now missing, but that owing to the weakened condition of the binding, they became loose and were lost.

Aside from the engraving on leaf 2, there are textual and typographical differences between the titlepages and preliminaries of the Madrid and Barcelona copies of this edition, and the same items in the Crosby copies. Although no major textual variants appear, and the different items are arranged as in the bibliographical description above, there are numerous differences in the use of italics and abbreviations, the correction of small errors, and the positioning of catchwords, headings, letters and lines. In the Madrid and Barcelona copies, for instance, the catchword at the bottom of leaf 3v is "Su-" (the first word of the *second* item on the following leaf is "Suma"), the titles of two printed books cited on leaf 4r are in italics, and on leaf 4v the word "folio" is written out in full. In the Crosby copies, however, the catchword is corrected to "Apro-" (the first word of the first item on the following leaf is "Aprobaciones"), there are no italicized titles on leaf 4r, and on leaf 4v the word "folio" is abbreviated to "Fol." Four small and easily corrected errors which appear in the Crosby copies ('sns' for 'sus,' 'algnn' for 'algun' on leaf 3r; 'tefiero' for 'refiero,' and 'lib.' for 'lin.' on leaf 4r), are corrected in the other two copies.

Unfortunately none of these differences offers really clear evidence of the filiation of the two sets of titlepages and preliminaries (even if the distribution of the errors were not contradictory, they are themselves of a type which would have been as easy to correct as to introduce).

The problem presented by signature x involves the lack in the Madrid, Barcelona, and Crosby (Ramírez de Arellano) copies of the last three leaves of this signature (x6, x7 and x8). In all copies of this edition, the recto of leaf x5, which is numbered as page 329, contains the end of the *Política de Dios,* and in the lower righthand corner there appears the catchword "VIDA." In the Crosby (Gigas) copy, the next page (leaf x6ʳ, page 331) contains the beginning of the *Vida de Marco Bruto.* The text of the *Marco Bruto* continues to the end of signature x (leaf x8ᵛ, page 336), where it breaks off in the middle of a sentence, and with no catchword. The next leaf, Y1ʳ, contains the beginning of a novel entitled *El perro y la calentura,* and is numbered as page 331. This novel is printed in full, and the new pagination continues consecutively to the end of the volume as if nothing had happened.

The explanation of this is that after the printer had run off signature x, which contained on its last three leaves the beginning of the *Marco Bruto,* he decided not to print the rest of this treatise (perhaps he felt it too long for the *Enseñanza entretenida*). Rather than setting up and printing all of signature x a second time, he began signature Y with *El perro y la calentura,* numbering the pages as they would have been numbered if the first three leaves of the *Marco Bruto* had not been printed. This pagination indicates that the printer intended to cut out the leaves containing the beginning of the *Marco Bruto,* but of course he could not do this until after the books had been stitched. The stubs of the cut pages are present in the Crosby (Ramírez de Arellano) copy, and can be seen clearly in the microfilm which I have of the Barcelona copy (in the film of the Madrid copy, the inner margins of pages 330 and 331 seem to be stuck together). The Crosby (Gigas) copy is one which somehow escaped the cutting operation.

There is one more feature of signature x which deserves comment: while in the Madrid copy and both Crosby copies leaf Y1ʳ is numbered as page 331, in the Barcelona copy it is numbered as page 337, surely because the compositor had in mind the number of the preceding page as originally printed, which was 336. The page following "337," however, is numbered 332, and thereafter the numbers continue in order. Evidently a few copies of signature Y were run off with the number 337, but the error was noticed and the type corrected to 331.

Edition K

(Madrid, 1648, Second 1648 Edition)

Titlepage: ENSEÑANÇA / ENTRETENIDA, / Y / DONAIROSA MO-RALIDAD, / Comprehendida / *En el Archiuo ingenioso de las Obras / escritas en Prosa,* / DE D. FRANCISCO DE QVEVEDO VILLE-GAS, / CAVALLERO DE LA ORDEN DE SANTIAGO, / I SEÑOR DE LA VILLA DE LA TORRE DE JVAN ABAD. / *Contienense juntas en este Tomo, las que sparcidas en diffe- / rentes Libros hasta aora se han / impresso.* / [A design] / EN MADRID, / Lo imprimiò EN SV OFFICINA DIEGO DIAZ / DE LA CARRERA. / [A line] / Año M.DC.XLVIII. / *A costa de Pedro Coello Mercader / de Libros.*

Colophon: None.

Preliminaries: Leaf 1r: titlepage. l. 1v: blank. l. 2r-2v: Dedication to Pedro Pacheco Girón, signed by Pedro Coello, undated. l. 3r: *Aprobaciones* by Diego del Carpio and Juan Vélez Zabala. *Suma de la licencia* by José de Arteaga, May 6, 1648. *Tasa* by José Arteaga, Madrid, June 22, 1648. *Erratas* by Carlos Murcia de la Llana, Madrid, June 20, 1648. l. 3v: Table of contents.

Text of the *Política de Dios:* Part I: twenty-four chapters, pp. 258-328, with neither preliminaries nor title (in the table of contents the title is listed as "Govierno superior de Dios, i Tirania de Satanas," which is a combination of the title of the first chapter and the title of the Zaragoza version).

Collation: [3] ff. + 1-394 pp. Errors in pagination: 31 (numbered as 30), 35 (as 53), 36 (as 39), 68 (as 98), 95 (as 65), 109 (as 106), 114 (as 141), 256 (as 526), 314 (as 214), 347-348 (as 349-350), 355-386 (as 354-385). Sigs. §⁴, B-I⁸, K-T⁸, V-Z⁸, Aa-Bb⁸, Cc⁴. Errors in signatures: Aa2 (numbered as A2), Aa3 (as A3). 19.7 × 13.8 cm.

Source of the text: edition B (first 1648 edition). The preliminaries of edition K share some typographical variants (but no errors) with those of the Madrid and Barcelona copies of edition B, and so may possibly have been copied from that set of preliminaries rather than from the set found in the Crosby copies of edition B.

Bibliographical descriptions: Fernández-Guerra, ed. Quevedo, *Política de Dios* (Madrid, 1867), I, p. xviii, note 1 (a brief reference).

Copies: Kongelige B. (Copenhagen). See also the Note on p. 118.

Madrid, 1650

a. Volume I

Titlepage: TODAS LAS / OBRAS EN PROSA / DE D. FRANCISCO
DE QVEVEDO / VILLEGAS, CAVALLERO DEL ORDEN / DE
SANTIAGO. / (SATIRICAS, POLITICAS, DEVOTAS) / Corregidas,
y de nueuo añadidas. / *A DON PEDRO SARMIENTO DE MEN-
DOZA,* / *Conde de Ribadauia, Adelantado de Galicia, de la Orden de*
/ *Calatraua.* / Año [An escutcheon] 1650. / Con Priuilegio, en Madrid
por Diego Diaz de la Carrera. / [A line] / *A costa de Tomas Alfai mer-
cader de libros.*

Colophon: None.

Preliminaries: folio [1]: titlepage. f. [2^r-2^v]: Dedication to Pedro Sarmiento de Mendoza, Conde de Ribadavia, signed by Tomás Alfay, undated. f. [3^r]: Table of contents, both of this volume and volume II.
f. [3^v]: *Aprobación* by Antonio Calderón, Madrid, June 22, 1644. f.
[4^r]:*Aprobación,* by Diego de Córdoba, Madrid, June 16, 1644, and
Licencia by Gabriel de Aldama, Madrid, June 16, 1644. f. [4^v]: *Suma
del Privilegio,* by Cañizares, Madrid, Dec. 17, 1648, and *Fe del Co-
rrector,* by Carlos Murcia de la Llana, Madrid, Feb. 8, 1650, and *Tasa,*
by Espadaña, Aug. 11, 1644.

Text of the *Política de Dios,* Part I: twenty-four chapters, pp. 100-175,
with neither preliminaries nor title.

Collation: [4] ff. + 1-252 pp. Errors in pagination: p. 58 (numbered as
38), 62 (as 60), 119 (as 116), 191 (as 119), 195 (as 165), 209-240 (as
281-312), 246 (as 247), 247 (as 246). Sigs. A-I^8, K-P^8, Q^4, R^2. Errors in
signatures: D2 (numbered as D3), E4 (as A4).

b. Volume II

Titlepage: PROSIGVEN / TODAS LAS / OBRAS EN PROSA / *DE D.
FRANCISCO DE QVEVEDO* / *Villegas, Cauallero del Orden de San-
tiago.* / *DEDICADO* / A don Gutierre Domingo de Teran Castañeda
Queuedo y Vi- / llegas señor de la casa de Teran, del valle de Yguña, /
montañas de Burgos. / Año [An escutcheon] 1650. / CON PRIVILE-
GIO, / *En Madrid. Por la viuda de Iuan Sanchez.* / A costa de Pedro
Coello, mercader de libros.

Colophon: CON PRIVILEGIO: / En Madrid, por Diego Diaz de la Carrera, / Año 1650.

Preliminaries: §1^r: titlepage. §1^v: blank. §2^r-4^r: Dedication to Gutierre
Domingo de Terán y Castañeda Quevedo y Villegas, Señor de la Casa
de Terán del valle de Yguña, montañas de Burgos. §4^v: *Aprobaciones*
by Diego del Carpio and Juan Vélez Zabala.

Collation: [4] ff. + 1-488 pp. Errors in pagination: p. 170 (numbered as

071), p. 287 (as 277). Sigs. §⁴, A-I⁸, K-T⁸, V⁸, X-Z⁸, Aa-Gg⁸, Hh⁴. Errors in signatures: Bb4 (as B4).

Source of the text of the *Política:* edition Q (1st Madrid, 1626).

Bibliographical descriptions: Fernández-Guerra, *BAE* XXIII, p. xcviii, col. c, no. 77; Astrana, *Verso,* p. 1391a (an abbreviated version of Fernández-Guerra's description); Amédée Mas, ed. Quevedo, *Las Zahurdas de Plutón* (Poitiers, [1956]), p. 29a, "Étude bibliografique." Professor Mas states that he has not seen this edition.

Copies (both volumes are bound together): Kongelige B. (Copenhagen), BN de Milano, BN Centrale (Florence), Library of the University of California in Los Angeles (California), B. Universitaria de Valladolid (this last is a very defective copy).

Madrid, 1655

Half-title: POLITICA / DE / DIOS, / Y / GOVIERNO / DE / CRISTO / NVESTRO SEÑOR.

Titlepage: a full-page engraving depicting a female figure which appears to be a composite of Thalia, the muse of comedy, and Melpomene, the muse of tragedy. Her arm rests on a long plaque containing the following title: "POLITICA DE DIOS, / I GOVIERNO DE X͞P͞O; / SACADA / DE LA SAGRADA ESCRI- / TVRA PARA ACIERTO / DE REY I REINO /EN SVS ACCIONES: / POR / Don Francisco De / Quevedo Villegas, / *Caballero de la Orden de* / *Santiago, Señor de la* / *Torre de Ioan Abad,* / *Marcos de O* [A portrait of Quevedo] *Orozco sculp.*" At the base of the engraving there is a much smaller plaque with the following legend: "*A Expensar* [sic] *de Pedro* / *Coello, en Madrid* / *Año de 1655.*" In the background there appears a seventeenth-century *corral de comedias,* and strewn at the feet of the muse is an assortment of theatrical masks and musical instruments.

Colophon: None.

Preliminaries: Leaf with neither number nor signature: half-title. a1ʳ: titlepage. a1ᵛ: blank. a2ʳ-a3ᵛ: Dedication to Antonio Juan Luiz de la Cerda, Duque de Medina Celín, signed by Pedro Coello, undated. a4ʳ-a4ᵛ: *Censura* by Pedro Luis de la Escalera, Madrid, Sept. 1, 1655. a5ʳ: *Censura* by Jerónimo Pardo, Madrid, June 5, 1652. a5ᵛ: *Suma de las Licencias,* Madrid, Sept. 7, 1654. *Tasa* by Francisco Espadaña, Madrid, Oct. 7, 1655. *Fe de Erratas* by Carlos Murcia, Madrid, Oct. 1, 1655. a6ʳ-a8ʳ: Table of contents. §1ʳ-§3ʳ: *Elogios* by Gil González, Cristóbal de Torres, Pedro de Urteaga, Gabriel de Castilla, and Lorenzo Vander Hammen. §4ʳ-§7ᵛ: Dedication to Pope Alexander VII, undated. §8ʳ-A1ʳ: "A los doctores sin luz, que dan humo en el pábilo muerto de sus censuras, muerden y no leen," and a quotation from St. Paul, I Corinthians, iii. 10-11. A1ᵛ: Quotations from Ecclesiastes, x, and Proverbs, vi. A2^r-A3^r: Dedication to Philip IV, signed by Quevedo. A3^v: Introduction to the First Part, with quotations from Wisdom, vi. *Text:* In two parts, with continuous pagination and signature numbers. Part I: text in twenty-four chapters, pp. 1-111. Part II: titlepage, p. 113; "A quien lee sanamente, y entiende assí lo que lee," pp. 115-119; "Palabras de la verdad para el desengaño de los reyes," with quotations from Wisdom, vii, pp. 119-120; "Prefación. A los hombres mortales que por el gran Dios de los exércitos tienen la tutela de las gentes desde el solio de la magestad: Pontífice, Emperador, Reyes, Príncipes," pp. 120-121. Text of Part II: twenty-three chapters, pp. 123-362.

Table of contents: see preliminaries, sigs. a6^r-a8^r.

Collation: [20] ff. + 1-362 pp. Errors in pagination: pp. 168, 169 (as 169, 170), 278 (as 277). Sigs. a^8, §^{8}, A-I^8, K-T^8, V-Z^8. 15.0 × 19.8 cm.

Source of the text: edition Q (1st Madrid, 1626).

Bibliographical descriptions: Fernández-Guerra, *BAE* XXIII, p. xcix, col. a, no. 81; Astrana, *Verso*, p. 1392b, no. 113.

Copies extant: Crosby (2 copies: one complete, one lacking the titlepage), Yale University Library (New Haven, Connecticut), Harvard College Library, one copy, and Harvard Law Library, another copy (Cambridge, Massachusetts), BN de Madrid (2 copies), B. de Menéndez Pelayo (Santander), B. Universitaria de Sevilla, B. Apostolica Vaticana (Rome), B. Ambrosiana (Milan), B. Casanatense (Rome), BN de Lisboa, B. de la Ville de Lyon, Kongelige B. (Copenhagen), Bayerische Staatsbibliothek (Munich), Österreichische Nationalbibliothek (Vienna).

In the engraving on the titlepage, the muse wears the tunic and laced boots with raised soles of Thalia, and in her left hand she carries the sceptre so carried by Melpomene. Thalia is usually depicted carrying theatrical masks in her hands, but here the masks lie at her feet. Perhaps this engraving was designed originally for a book connected with the theatre, and was later used by the printer of the *Política*, who inserted the two plaques.

The copies of this edition in Seville and Vienna are sometimes assigned the date of 1699, an error no doubt caused by the somewhat unusual shape of the last two digits of the date 1655 as engraved on the titlepage. Of the two copies in the BN de Madrid, one, R/31586, contains several pages which are torn, and the other, R/5322, lacks the titlepage and is sometimes erroneously assigned the date of 1656.

Note to pp. 113-115: As these lines go to press, my good friend Professor Elias L. Rivers generously informs me that he has just identified in the BN de Madrid another copy of edition B (numbered U/652), and another of ed. K (R/17321). The "Madrid copy" of B mentioned on p. 113 is R/7767.

INDEX

Biblioteca, Bibliothèque, Bibliotek, etc., are abbreviated below as B.
Boldface type below indicates principles of textual criticism.

119